Doing GOD'S Will

"A Memoir"

ESTHER JAMES

WESTBOW
PRESS®
A DIVISION OF THOMAS NELSON
& ZONDERVAN

WestBow Press books may be ordered through booksellers or by contacting:

WestBow Press
A Division of Thomas Nelson & Zondervan
1663 Liberty Drive
Bloomington, IN 47403
www.westbowpress.com
844-714-3454

Scripture taken from the New King James Version® Copyright © 1982 by Thomas Nelson. Used by permission. All rights reserved.

ISBN: 978-1-6642-0421-8 (sc)
ISBN: 978-1-6642-0422-5 (e)

Library of Congress Control Number: 2020916876

Print information available on the last page.

WestBow Press rev. date: 11/25/2020

CONTENTS

INTRODUCTION

Have you ever felt like God didn't love you? Have you ever felt condemned because of your past and like God has not forgiven you? Do you feel like you have not forgiven yourself? Have you ever felt like because of your past mistakes and sins that God could not use you? With God, there is now no condemnation (Romans 8:1 NKJV). With countless sins and mistakes, what I have found through the testimony of my life is that God can use anybody He desires to use. I do believe that the enemy "meant evil against me; but God meant it for good…" (Genesis 50:20 NKJV). I believe that He uses those who have messed up the most to do His will so that He can get glory out of their lives.

As I wrote this book, I ventured over my life from childhood until now. I discuss my personal experiences associated with my childhood, college years, relationships with men, adulthood, as a single-parent mom, and when God told me to move. Your parents give you life, but God gives you your destiny for life. I speak about various life experiences. From the thinkable to the unthinkable, I have sinned in countless ways. Despite my countless fallacies, God still desired to use me. He decided to turn my mistakes and misery into a powerful ministry to help others. You cannot help others if you have never been through anything. How can you minister to someone who is a single parent mom when you have never been one? How can you minister to someone promiscuous if you have not walked in that person's shoes? How can you comfort someone who has lost, not one, but both parents, if that has not happened to you? Your perspective changes when you go through things. The way you talk to people changes what you say and how you say it. Your view of people and their emotions or actions revolving around moments of their lives changes because you can empathize. You learn to show grace and mercy as you've never shown people before. Ultimately, you learn to stop being so judgmental. "[F]or all have sinned and fall short of the glory of God (Romans 3:23 NKJV). So, what sins have you committed?

CHAPTER I

Childhood

My paternal grandfather died before I was born. I always heard stories about my grandfather. I wish I would have met him, but death waits for no one. A beautiful baby girl was born days after his passing. Yes, I said beautiful. If I don't say to myself that I am beautiful, then who will?

God has had me covered ever since I was a baby. God would wake my maternal grandfather up the same time every morning. My maternal grandmother repetitively talked about how he used to rise early in the morning around 3 or 4 o'clock to care for me. He always made certain that I was taken care of and had provision. I always felt safe around my grandfather and at peace in his presence. My grandfather must have known that God had a plan for my life.

When I was younger, I always felt like the people I loved the most were dying. I remember being mad at my dad because he would not take me to see one of my cousins in the hospital who had leukemia. My cousin was so full of life and always made people laugh. When I finally saw my cousin after his hospital stay, I felt dreadful. I did not go and see him in the hospital. Though it was beyond my control, I felt as though I had deserted him. When he died, it bothered me.

When my maternal grandfather passed, I cried profusely. I was around 8 or 10 years old at the time. I was upset with my cousin because I thought that he could have done something to save my grandfather's life. As I grew older, I realized that was not the case. I just wanted my grandfather back.

It was around this time that I recall seeing a vision of what I believed to be Jesus. When I attended my grandfather's funeral, they sang, "What A Friend We Have in Jesus". That song has stuck with me all these years. I vowed even then I would not forget that song.

During my early years, my grandfather would spoil me. When he took his insulin shots, he would pretend he was going to stick me with the needle. I miss my grandfather proclaiming truisms of wisdom. When we used to fall off our bikes, he would utter, "Dust yourself off and get back up again." I recall conveying to a couple of guys what my grandfather declared. As I became older, I recognized that this cliché could be applied to life.

My grandfather and I had a mutual love for one another. He never spanked me. My sister and I tussled over a chair I had been sitting in. My grandfather got his belt out. I was petrified. My grandfather gave my sister a spanking so bad that I could feel her pain. I thought that he was going to spank me next. Thank God! He didn't. I knew I was the apple of his eye and that I was special to him. Not only did my grandfather spoil me, but my maternal grandmother did as well. She would hide chitterlings for me and tell her children she did not have anymore. She would tell me to be quiet and hand me a plate of chitterlings that she hid just for me. Oh, how I miss those days.

When we were little, my siblings and I stayed with my maternal grandparents on the weekends. My grandmother continually made certain that we attended church. My grandmother ensured that all her children, grandchildren, and great-grandchildren attended church when they stayed at her house. We were in the sanctuary every time the doors of the church were open. We rose early on Sunday morning to eat breakfast and walked down to the church. My grandmother taught Sunday School, so she taught us. After Sunday School, we would venture off to my great-grandmother's house to get some snacks to eat, but we had to be back for the regular church service. We sang in the children's choir. We also said our speeches when it was Easter and Christmas. We traveled on church trips and youth outings. We also attended Vacation Bible School. Nightly, we would kneel by the bedside and pray.

My maternal grandmother loved us unconditionally, whether we exhibited acceptable or unacceptable behavior. She would correct us in love. She showed us grace and mercy. She was an epitome of God's agape love. I believe that my grandmother had spiritual gifts and could see us through God's lenses. I adored being around her. She would offer tidbits of sage and wisdom. She would say things like, "You have to listen to somebody" and "You reap what you sow".

My grandmother and my great-aunt always knew the right words to say when I visited them in their nursing homes. I knew that they were saying what God told them to say. There were times when I would not say anything, and they would say the right words I needed to hear. When I went to visit my grandmother one night at the nursing home, I recall her telling me to always stay out in front in whatever I set my mind to do. She also told me that she knew that my mom was going to die. By the time she told me, I was mature enough to handle it. My great-aunt told me that everything was going to be alright. How did she know? I did not tell her what I was going through at the time. But God.

I was able to spend some time with my paternal grandmother. My dad would take us over there and spend countless hours conversing with my grandmother about various matters. I spent more time with her when I became an adult. I would go to her house and listen to her words of wisdom. I would discuss my relationships with her. I remember her telling me to stay the way I was, and she wished that I would meet someone nice.

As time went on, I remember receiving salvation and being water baptized at the age of 13. Inquisitively, my aunt wanted to know if I was knowledgeable about the significance of the water baptism. My dad didn't appear to be too happy about it and wasn't very supportive. That is when the opposition began.

I was sitting in church one Sunday as usual. My parents came and got me out of the church because my uncle accused me of stealing his money. That was one of the worse days of my life. We went home and looked through the dirty clothes hamper to find the clothes I had on the previous day. My parents inspected the pockets and found no money. I told my parents I did not pilfer the money and told them that my cousin did. My aunt showed us where the money was and told me to get the money. I refused to do so. Then, she told my cousin, her daughter, to snatch the money, and my cousin complied. I was so petrified that I could have urinated in my pants.

When my parents realized that I was being truthful, my dad let his family have it with a few choice words. After that, we did not go over to my paternal grandmother's house or my dad's other family members' houses for a long time. Frankly speaking, my dad held a grudge, and it took some time for him to forgive his family. To this day, I still recollect that experience like it happened yesterday. I have occasionally mentioned it. It's ironic how occurrences from our childhood can remain entrenched in our adult minds.

As a youngster, I lived in a house where there was domestic abuse that occurred between my parents. I was always the cry baby. I didn't like to see my parents fight. You would have thought that I was the youngest in the family. We, the children, were never physically abused. We were just spanked like normal children for unacceptable behavior or grounded. What was abnormal to others became normal to us. The domestic abuse became second nature. My desire was for my parents to get a divorce so that I could live with my dad. Every time they would separate, we would have to go with my mom to my grandparents' house. I would cry until I arrived there to see my grandfather.

My parents would have one big scuffle annually it seemed. I remember one time my mom had an ashtray lodged against my dad's head. He always talked about how she was trying to kill him. My dad had served in the Vietnam War and received the Purple Heart medal. He had a plate in his head due to his stint in the Vietnam War. He would talk about how one of his friends saved his life and how he encountered a near-death experience.

I believe that my dad suffered from post-traumatic stress disorder. At one of my birthday parties, my dad became so irate that he shattered the back window of my mom's car. The glass exploded everywhere. Another attack occurred one night after we had retired to bed. Awakened by the screaming and yelling, I remember rising to my mom holding a chair, and my dad clutching a knife tightly in his hand. That night, my sister and I took my mom with a gash in her arm to the hospital, while my brother took my dad to the same hospital with a bump on his head. What a night!

Don't get me wrong. My parents were great parents to us. They just had problems with each other. They were functional in their dysfunction. Our parents would make certain that we excelled in school. We all made Honor Roll in school. For the most part, we were well-behaved and said,

"Yes ma'am", "No ma'am", "Yes sir", and "No sir". We were raised right. They raised us with morals and values. They believed in what was right. They stood by you if you were right. They let you know that if you were wrong, they would beat you like you stole something. My dad would go to the school and conference with the teachers if we had any problems in the classroom. If he did not receive the results he desired, he would conference with the principal. If the principal did not provide the results he desired, he would threaten to meet with the superintendent. Usually, the problem was resolved with the principal.

My parents supported me when I was involved in extracurricular activities. They supported me when I played basketball by attending the games. They were present at my marching band competitions. Additionally, they attended my award banquets and ceremonies.

Both of my parents were involved with the youth. My dad coached baseball, football, and basketball at the local YMCA. He was a great coach and loved the kids. The parents and kids loved my dad as well. My mom was a school teacher who taught at the local high school where we all attended school. She loved her students, and they loved her too. She even taught me how to type in Typing I.

Although my mom got along well with her students, my mom and I did not get along. I felt like my mom despised me. When I was younger, I remember my mom used to say that I was crazy just like my dad. I did not feel close to my mom. She and I would disagree about trivial matters, like calling something a cup or a glass. I remember a time I called her mommy, and she looked at me with disdain. I look back at those moments now and shake my head. What a waste of precious time! My dad attributed our inability to get along to our similar strong personalities.

I did not care for my mom. My dad and I always felt like she was trying to drive a wedge between us. My dad and I used to sit in the car and have a discussion about her. My dad would say that we were too much alike. Now that I am older, I do see some similar characteristics. My mom and I loved acquiring an education and were determined to complete our educational endeavors. We did not let anything stop us, not even bearing children. We were both obstinate and determined.

I remember telling my dad I wanted to learn how to do the laundry. He wanted my mom to show me. In my mind, that was going to be the worst experience ever. I decided I didn't want to learn anymore because my mom was the one who was going to teach me. However, my dad wanted us to establish a bond. Nevertheless, I learned with the help of my mom's guidance. Surprisingly, it ended up being a pleasant experience.

My father was a great dad. He was fun to be around. I loved doing things with him. He had patience. I learned how to cook hanging out with him in the kitchen. He loved to cook meals and bake cakes. His specialty was his 7-Up cake. My dad and I would engage in intimate conversations. The only things I could not talk to him about were boys and feminine issues. No boy was ever good enough for me. That's why I think that I am over 40 now with no husband and unmarried. I will say that my father taught me about having standards. My standards were high. I always remembered the wise words of my father when dating or being in a relationship with a guy. His sage got me out of some toxic relationships. My dad and I would sit in the car and have discussions about my mom. He always believed that she wanted him to discipline me to create a wedge between us because we shared a strong father-daughter bond.

Because my mom used to say that I was crazy, I believed that my siblings shared similar thoughts. Yeah, I did some crazy things, but I'm not crazy. For a while, I enjoyed the fact that people thought that I was crazy. They would leave me alone and not bother me. It's ironic how words people have spoken over you take root to where you believe them. I had to change the way I viewed myself from the words my dad and mom spoke over me. They did not have a relationship with God at the time. I think that my mom was starting to change by religiously attending church, but my dad was set in his ways. I believe that my dad was hurt by church people, so he stopped attending church.

I recall having my menstrual. I was so embarrassed and felt like I could not talk to my mom or dad about it. I would obtain feminine products from one of my classmates. My mom was washing laundry one day and discovered that I was experiencing my menstrual and inquired about it. She asked me why I did not tell her. Why would I? We did not have a close relationship. I certainly was not going to discuss it with my dad. Embarrassing!

When it came to my mom, I did not like the way she would speak to my maternal grandmother. She was so rude towards my grandmother.

Unknowingly, I saw a generational curse before my eyes and was a part of it myself. My mom did not get along with her mom, nor did I get along with my mom. After I became a mother, my daughter and I had issues of our own.

When I went to college, my mom left my dad. My mom and I began to build a better relationship with one another. She was amicable. We were unable to continue that relationship because of her untimely death. It was not until after her death that I learned that she cohabited with another man. I say that not to discredit my mom's character, but to inform you that I met with this man after I had my children. He was very friendly. I even met his mom, who was courteous as well. He took me out to eat and blessed me with some money. He wanted me to keep in touch, but I chose not to do so. He told me that my mom was proud of me and knew that I would do well in life. I was astonished. I felt like my mom hated me because of the way she treated me. She always favored my siblings, especially my brother. My brother was my mom's favorite. I'm not complaining because I was my dad's favorite. I guess that is why I could so easily forgive my dad for killing my mom and then killing himself. The lingering issue that I had was with my mom. I had to sort through those feelings. I was dating this guy at the time, and we attended church. It was Mother's Day. The pastor talked about loving your mother. I didn't know if I loved my mom. My live-in boyfriend reassured me that I loved my mom. It took me some time to deal with that issue, but I realized that I did love my mom. It was just an uncanny and somewhat disaffected relationship. My expectations for a mother-daughter relationship were unfulfilled.

Reminiscing, my mom was distant. I could tell that she was a hurt person. It wasn't until later on in life that my aunt revealed some things about my mom's life. My mom had issues with my grandmother. My grandfather would tell my grandmother to send my mom money while she was in college, but my grandmother would spend the money on herself. As a result, my mom felt hurt by my grandfather, until she found out the truth. Then, she detested my grandmother. I also found out that my mother became pregnant in college. Did she have an abortion or a miscarriage? When she left my dad, she cohabited with another man. She was going on secret rendezvous with him. Was she regretting not being with the love of her life? When I met with this mystery man, he told me that he loved my mom and always did. He named one of his daughters after my mom. I don't know what transpired between him and my mom, but I felt as though they had always loved each other. They just took the wrong paths to love.

If I could be transparent, I felt as though my mom's actions affected me. I recall not desiring to be in a committed relationship because I was fearful that I was going to turn out like my mom. I did not want to be married and have regrets. I did not want to cheat on my husband. As such, I do not attribute me not being married solely being my dad's fault. I do not make these comments about my mom to discredit her character, but just to reveal my truths. What a parent does or does not do affects the children they give life.

Our house was a house divided. It was my dad and me and then there were my mom and my siblings. I believe that the division my siblings and I experience today is due to our home life. As much as I have attempted to bring our family together with Thanksgiving dinners, the division still exists. My siblings and I do not have the kind of relationship I wish we had similar to other loving families.

As I matured spiritually, I learned that the spirit of familial division began well before my parents existed. It existed in their families. On my mom's side, she and her siblings were paired up. On my dad's side, they always kept strife and confusion going. Those are the generational curses pastors preach about. As much as I might have wanted unity in our family, I learned that everyone has to be willing to participate.

I loved family time. But at times, I hated spending time with my family. They would always bring up the past harboring unforgiveness. There were some family members in attendance who had beef with each other. Family can be petty and childish no matter the age of the person. Backbiting, unforgiveness, greed, poverty, gossiping, holding grudges, envy, jealousy, pride, and sense of entitlement were some of the sins that plagued our family bloodlines.

I did have some good times with my family. When I was 15 years old, I would go riding with my cousins. Sometimes, they had me in the housing projects going to see guys whom they were interested in. One day, they went looking for employment opportunities. We went to a fast-food restaurant. They suggested that I apply for a job as well. Needless to say, I filled out a job application. Days later, I received a phone call. The manager asked someone did he hire me. I heard someone in the background say, "Yes." Next thing you know, I was on the work schedule. My cousin said that she was the one who affirmed that they hired me. I started working at this restaurant as a cashier and cook. I'll have to admit that I enjoyed discreetly eating the chicken nuggets fresh out of the hot oven and hot fries coming out of the hot oil. I loved that job. Then, I finally moved to a job closer to home as a cashier at a nearby grocery store.

During my senior year, I worked at the local bank. Since my mom was a business education teacher and a club advisor, the branch manager asked my mom if she knew anyone who wanted to work at the bank after school. She asked me if I wanted to take advantage of this job opportunity. I said, "Yes." I was a bookkeeper and a teller. I enjoyed working at the bank. I opened up my first checking account and received my first credit card with a $500 limit. At the time, I didn't know that my mom had placed me as an authorized user on her store credit card and was working to help me build my credit. I did the same thing with my children to help them build their credit. It helped them and me when we went to make our purchases on credit.

As a student, I was stellar at school. I made the Honor Roll most of my academic years, except one nine weeks when I made a C in third grade. I was devastated and disappointed with myself. I vowed to myself that I would never make a C again. In high school, a football player would tease me and call me, "Nerd of the year". Consciously, I thought that I would rather be a nerd than a dumb jock. I was the laughing stock of other students' witticisms as the "nerd" in school. People always raved about how smart and intelligent I was.

For the most part, I was angelic at school but nefarious at home. I remember placing a sharp pencil on a car seat, and my brother sat on it. Needless to say, he had a pencil lead in his rump. I don't know what I was thinking. I guess I thought it was a prank. It was a hoax that almost cost me my dear life.

When my parents went somewhere, I would stay at home and take the car to visit boys. I would try to get back before my parents arrived back home. Well, one day, I did not get back on time. I got in so much trouble. If you haven't realized it by now, I was the troubled child at home. I would lie and tell my dad I was talking to a female friend on the phone when I was talking to a boy. My dad would delude me into telling the truth. Several times, I think he was calling my bluff.

I detested attending the same high school where my mom worked. Every time they called me to the office, she had to know the reason for the office visit. Most of the time, it was for something good. One day, I made a poor choice to damage my impeccable record by pushing my friend into another student. The principal called me to the office. He asked me why I did such a deplorable thing. I frankly told him that it was because I did not like the student. She was sitting in the office while I shared my truth. After exiting the principal's office, I overheard the principal tell my mom that I was an honest student. I did not receive any punishment at school. When I arrived home, I had to listen to a lecture from my parents.

After school one day, I sat in the car waiting for my mom to come out. Adhering to peer pressure, one of my friends asked me did I know how to drive. In trying to prove to her that I could drive, a mishap occurred. Well, I crashed into my science teacher's car and damaged it. I thought I had escaped punishment until my dad detected the damage to the car after we had arrived home. I confessed to my devilish act. My mom took me over to my science teacher's house and compelled me to apologize. My science teacher was understanding. However, my parents were not. Of course, I was punished.

One night, my dad permitted me to use his car to go to a football game. He told me to be home by 11 PM. Well after considering the possible punishment, I decided to go home around 11:30 PM. Everyone else was going to hang out after the game. I wanted to be like everybody else. Back then, we did not have cell phones as we do now. On the way home, I thought I saw my dad pass by me. Well, when I arrived home, his car was missing from the driveway. I knew I was in for a nice treat. When my dad arrived back home, I had to hear his lecture. I was rolling my eyes. I was tired of the lectures, but I kept doing things to receive the lectures. Let's just say, I was always walking around in the wilderness. After my parents died, I remembered everything my dad had said. Those words of sage and wisdom have helped me tremendously in life. I even told my grandmother that I felt like I was the one who listened the most out of all of us. Well, I was the one who caused my siblings and me to sit through countless lectures due to my poor decision making. Truthfully speaking, I do remember everything my parents spoke and have tried to apply it to my life from homeownership and finances to relationships and integrity. Suitably, I hold my dad partially culpable for me not being married. I have realized that when a girl has a phenomenal dad who spoiled her, it makes it difficult for the guy who pursues her. That girl maintains high standards.

When I was in high school, I had somewhat of a crush on a cool guy who was older than me. I was a quiet and observant student in school. I would sit at the cafeteria table and hardly say a word. Well, one night at a football game, I remember this cool guy persuading me to go with him. He asked me to meet him outside of the game. I thought that maybe we were going to talk, and, at the most, kiss. I was still young but in high school. Naively, I went with him. Well, it turned out to be a life-changing moment for me and a rude awakening. He convinced me to walk to the back of a school bus. I felt coerced by him to perform a sexual act. It was not what I wanted to do, but he made me feel like I had to perform this act with his threatening words. Needless to say, my parents found out. My dad confronted me. I told him what happened. My parents pressed charges. The criminal offense was statutory rape or sexual assault. We ended up going to court. Because of the pressure of the interrogation and my father's words, I became confused. We ended up losing the case. My parents were irate. I just wanted it to end. I was so embarrassed. Even though we did not win the case, I still believe that God vindicated me even in that situation because that guy did not live a good life afterward. It's ironic how we suppress things of our past experiences out of our remembrance to face them in our adult years.

In my younger days, we were sent into a room to go play or played outside with other children. We could not sit in the house around adults and listen to their conversations. When the spirit of perversion entered into my life, I was young. It's incomprehensible how you remember childhood moments as an adult. During my childhood, I have been touched inappropriately during those moments of playing. These acts led to my desire to masturbate. Back then, they would say colloquialisms like, "What goes on in our house stays in our house." Not to mention, my parents were very strict. I did not feel as though I could discuss important issues with my parents. I could discuss casual matters with my dad, but not the deep things of what I was experiencing. I felt like my parents just did not understand.

During my senior year of high school, my sister and I thought we were grown. We were disrespectful to our parents. We tried to pack our clothes and run away from home. My dad said take what you bought. As you know, that was not much. I forgot what the argument was about. I just know we used the neighbor's phone to call our cousin. We sat at the end of the driveway and went and stayed at my aunt's and uncle's house for a few days. When we arrived back home, my mom told us how our aunt had come to the school and wanted them to take us back. My parents were more willing to take my sister back than me. I couldn't comprehend why at the time because my sister was the sassier and mouthier one. They finally decided to let me back in the house. I recall treading lightly when I first arrived. Nonetheless, I anticipated the moment for me to attend college and get out of that house.

While my mother was sanitizing the pool, I sat in the back yard beside my dad on a bench. I told my dad that I wanted to be the top person in my graduating class. I did not know the term at the time. My mom said, "Valedictorian." Why did I tell them my plans? Well, my mom pestered me about my grades and would inquire about other students' grades. I didn't know. I just focused on myself and stayed in my lane. My mom would become infuriated because I did not know other students' grades. I thought that she was ludicrous. Even to this day, I have learned to mind my own business. It has proved to be quite successful for me. After much focus, discipline, and diligence on my part, I ended up being valedictorian of my graduating class. I was elated at the fact that I had achieved a goal I had set for myself. I look back at that moment now and see how I had favor. "Death and life are in the power of the tongue..." (Proverbs 18:21 NKJV). If you speak it, it shall come to pass.

What bothered me about my moment of victory was that I recognized that not everyone is for you. Just because you desire to be celebrated by others does not mean that will happen. I remember another black female student in our graduating class accosting me and telling me how she was displeased by the fact that I was graduating as the valedictorian. I extended no reply to her declaration. Who would have ever contemplated that one would have the audacity to do such a thing? As time passed by and we matured, that same female came back to me and said that she wished that she would have applied herself more in school. She believed that her life would have turned out differently. Look at God! "And we know that all things work together for good to those who love God, to those who are the called according to His purpose" (Romans 8:28 NKJV). He will "make your enemies your footstool" (Psalm 110:1 NKJV).

I longed to attend college. I had countless offers. Thank God for the academic scholarships that God blessed me with to attend college. I was adamant about attending one particular university. I had attended a camp there during the summer and cherished my experience. I remember my dad proclaiming that if I attended this particular university, he would not come to visit me. He did not like the historical associations linked to this university. Needless to say, I was fine with that. As I began to ponder over my decision, I conceded that the university comprised most of its town. I did not want to attend a university in a small town. I came from a small town, so I chose to attend a university in a big college town. It was the best decision I had ever made. My best years of schooling occurred while I attended this university. I loved it there. I partied, attended football games, and had a great social life. Now, I could have applied myself more academically, but I cherished my time there. I savored my college years better than my high school years. When I step on college campuses now as an adult, I reminisce about the good times of college days.

The same year I graduated from high school and began my college academic career, tragedy hit my family. I went home for Thanksgiving, and my parents were separated. My dad and I ended up getting into a squabble because I took my brother's side to find out that my dad was correct about my brother. My siblings and I ended up staying with my cousin. I wished that I would have conferred with my dad before I left.

The day my parents died was a turning point in my life. I thought I heard my roommate yell my name. I was mad at her and was studying for my final exams in the study room. When I finally went back into the room, she told me that my sister called from my uncle's house. I began to cry. I knew that something was wrong because my sister called me from my uncle's house. We hardly ever stayed anywhere else besides our parents' house. With anticipation, I called my uncle's house. My cousin answered the phone and said that he was going to let my sister tell me. I knew that something was wrong. My sister got on the phone and told me that our parents were deceased and provided the details surrounding their deaths. My dad had shot my mom and killed himself. I cried profusely. At that very moment, my world shattered.

After receiving the news from my sister over the phone, I waited for my ride to pick me up. In the meantime, I remember my friend and I walking around on campus and everyone extending their condolences. Everyone was so cordial and sympathetic. At the time, I didn't know that I was in denial. I recollect looking at my brother and wondering why he was crying profusely. It took time for my parents' deaths to sink in. I thought that it was a joke that my parents were playing on us to see if we cared. It wasn't until we went to view their bodies that I realized that my parents were deceased. I remember looking at my dad's hand and seeing the scar on his hand. I said, "This really is my dad."

People thought that I was supposed to be mad at my dad. I was more upset with them because they thought that I was supposed to be mad at my dad. I loved my dad. I was a daddy's girl. Nothing he did was going to change that. I believe that what occurred between him and my mom was just that, between him and my mom. I knew that our parents loved us. They just couldn't get along.

I remember my dad telling me to attend church the Sunday before he and my mom died. I did not go because I was tired. After he and my mom died, I faulted myself for not attending church. I thought that maybe that would have made a difference in the outcome of my parents' deaths. Why didn't I just get up and go to church? I also thought that if I would have been there my parents would still be alive today. I thought that maybe I could have been the one to talk my dad out of shooting my mom and himself. When I became an adult, the Holy Spirit let me know that it was not my fault. Following their deaths, we found a note that my dad left. He did not want us to hurt anymore.

Afterward, I prayed to God and asked Him for wisdom, knowledge, and understanding. I knew that God heard my prayer because he granted it to me. After my parents died, I had to handle both of their estates. I felt like family was a nuisance and just wanted to be meddlesome. They tried to get us to sell our house to live closer to them. I'm so glad that we didn't. Why would you want us to pay higher taxes to live?

There was mass confusion. The information was overwhelming. Uncles were planning meetings that they did not discuss with me. How are you going to orchestrate consultations without the executor of the estates knowing about it? Everyone had an opinion, but we felt like our family was unconcerned about our feelings, our welfare, and the fact that we had just lost both of our parents.

How would you feel if you found out that both of your parents died the same day? How would you feel if you were attending a double funeral? Until you have walked a mile in a person's shoes, don't judge them. Don't offer any advice. Just pray for them in your prayer closet. I know people did not mean any harm, but they could not empathize. It's not until you have a parent or someone close to you die that you can even begin to comprehend.

Some of our family members were our worst enemies. I sensed that our family was only concerned about our financial situation. I felt like family members were taking advantage of my siblings financially. We did not mind paying. We just wanted them to charge a fair price for them to reside with them. We had just lost both of our parents. When my parents died, I understood the meaning of the scripture, "For the love of money is a root of all kinds of evil..." (1 Timothy 6:10 NKJV).

As a result, I hated going home. One of my uncles wanted me to transfer to a college nearby. That was out of the question. God had us in the palm of His hands.

CHAPTER 2

College Years

After high school ended, I was counting down the days to go off to college. I could not wait to get out of my parents' house. When I went off to college, I was ecstatic. I arrived to college to experience a new chapter in my life.

My roommate was someone I had met while we attended a summer camp together. I enjoyed my college life. I felt as though I was free to roam. I partied from Thursday night until Saturday night. I attended all the sorority and fraternity parties in addition to the off-campus parties. I would hardly ever go home. During breaks, I would venture to Atlanta, Georgia. I traveled endlessly to Atlanta. One of my roommate's moms suggested that I move to Atlanta.

When my parents would come to visit me in college, I remember when my dad would call me out of my name indicating that I was being promiscuous. I was not doing anything. I recollect thinking that if he is accusing me of it, then why not do it. During my freshman year of college, I decided to fornicate with one of the college guys. I just wanted to see what the thrill of relations was about. I did not understand what the hoopla was about. Yes, I would take my dad's car to go see guys when I was younger. I never engaged in sexual intercourse or any type of sex act with the guys. The guys always said that I was a tease. You never know what seed is being spoken over your life until it takes root.

As college life progressed, I found myself having sex with a guy from another ethnicity. Myths about others are inaccurate. Yes, I became promiscuous. I remember having a Tim #1 and Tim #2. I also had a Brian #1 and Brian #2. Don't get it twisted. I did not have sex with everyone I came in contact with. I would receive free HIV testing when it was offered. Sad, but true. I realized that I was just trying to fill a void in my life, especially after my parents passed away.

Then, I finally met my children's father. Though it was my choice, God will send you a lesson that you will never forget. I decided to date someone who was not what God had for me and then dared to have children with him. What was I thinking? Now, I overlooked all these college guys to end up with someone who was not doing much with his life. I just liked the thrill of traveling and new adventures. I wanted the bad boy. Listen ladies, bad boys are not what you want. You want a good man who has a vision and a God-given purpose for his life. I wish someone would have told me that.

Before I could finish my freshmen year in college, my parents died. At the time, I had a relentless English professor, who wanted me to attend counseling. I would always tell her that I would attend counseling, but I wouldn't. Finally, I got tired of her asking me, so I went. I wish that I could remember her name and go back and thank her. She helped me at a pivotal moment in my life with her advice. Hence, I attended counseling and was educated about the various stages of grief. I discovered that I enjoyed the counseling sessions. In the black community, a stigma is attached to going to see a psychologist or counselor. It turned out that counseling transformed me from a quiet, timid person to one who began to express her feelings vociferously. I learned that as much as I can sit quietly in a room and just observe is as much as I can express myself vocally when I need to do so. The counselor conveyed to me that it was unhealthy to retain my feelings and that I needed to openly express myself. Boy, did I comply?

During my senior year of college, I made up in my mind that I wanted to become pregnant. And pregnant, I became. I walked around campus with a big belly with not one, but two babies. I was alright with the possibility of one child, but two. Wow!

When I decided to become pregnant, I did not consider all the details and consequences associated with this decision. The twins came earlier than anticipated. When my children came out of NICU, I had already begun the last semester to finish up college.

I did not have a great support system. It was by the grace of God that I found a babysitter. I needed someone who could keep my children during the week, and I would come home on the weekends to care for my children. The first babysitter was not a good one. It did not sit right in my spirit to let them stay with the first babysitter. Then, I had to find another babysitter. The next babysitter was phenomenal with my children. She treated my children like they were her own. I was starting to get a little jealous at times, but she was good to my children. I needed help to finish my degree. Only a couple of months left. I needed for my children to be with someone I could trust.

After much turmoil, I finally finished my college education. I felt a sense of achievement, especially after having my children. My maternal grandmother, my uncle, and my children attended my graduation. What a great feat! I had to finish not only for myself, but for my kids as well. I wanted to create a legacy and pass on generational blessings.

CHAPTER 3

Relationship with Men

I encountered my first true love while I was at a summer camp. We used to stroll along the water. We ventured off to an ice cream parlor and affectionately served each other ice cream. We would amorously embrace hands. He wrote me poetry laced with doting lingo and sketched my face with vivid detail. His oeuvre was impeccable. We also danced together in a group and had a dance exhibition of our moves.

When we parted, he presented me with a single yellow rose. I treasured that rose. Regrettably, I left the rose in the hotel room when my family and I went on vacation. When I realized it, my dad would not allow me to go back into the room to retrieve it. I was upset with my dad and wept over the loss of a cherished gift.

After we left the summer camp, I tried to keep in touch with the love of my life. It turns out that the feelings were not mutual. I was heartbroken. I knew that he wanted to take our relationship to another level, but I wasn't ready for that yet. My dad always told me that if a man loves you he will wait. I also knew that he was stuck on a girl from back home, but I opened up my heart to him thinking that he was trying to move on. Ladies, when a man is still hung up on another female, run and spare your feelings.

At some point in my teenage life, the spirit of rejection set in. When I thought that a guy was going to dump me, I would dump him first. I did not want to be rejected.

My parents' rule was that we could take suitors at the house when we were 15 years of age and go on dates when we were 16 years old. Well, a guy asked me out while I was working at the local bank. He was about 8 or 10 years my senior. I asked my parents if I could date him. Surprisingly, they allowed me to do so. He took me out, but we ended up at his place. I let him know that I was not ready for sexual relations. I continued to date him when I went off to college and would take him around my male friends. I felt indifferent about his feelings. I was so self-involved and egocentric at the time. He wanted to buy me a car, but my roommate talked me out of it. She let me know that was an attempt for him to control me. I declined the offer. Needless to say, our relationship did not work out. Little did I know, that God was working things out for my good (Romans 8:28 NKJV). He ended up losing his job.

I dated a guy who played college basketball. I felt as though he had great potential. My dad used to talk about his car. He said that it doesn't matter what kind of car a man has just as long as he keeps it clean. According to my dad, the cleanliness of a man's car and his shoes were analogous to a man's character. I never comprehended it. Years later, that same guy ended up in a bad situation. When my father died, I remembered everything he told me about guys.

At times, I was emotionally detached from the guys I associated myself with in college. I remember a gentleman who was courteous to me. He would spoil me and give me anything that I requested. I was an ingrate and took him for granted. I messed things up by opening my big mouth and asserting, "When I say jump, you say how high." I have regretted that moment in my adult life. That could have been my husband. If only my parents would have conferred with me more about life and relationships in more detail.

I also remember my ex-boyfriend's college roommate desiring to be with me. I thought that he was a nice guy, but he scared me with his acts of desperation. I just did not believe in being with a guy's friends or family members after I had dated or been in a relationship with him.

I remember meeting a nice guy who lived off-campus. By that time, I was so stuck on my children's father. I remember him saying that my children should have been his children. Maybe, they should have been. They would have been better off. My children and I ended up staying with him when I returned to my college town to start my new life. It was when I returned, that my life took a new trajectory into a better life.

My children's father and I met while my cousin was staying at my parents' house with my brother. We needed someone to stay with my brother since he was under the age of 18. My sister and I were away in college. My cousin and my children's father hung out with each other. They were both "bad boys". I loved my cousin. My cousin needed to get away from his toxic environment. Since my children's father was over there often, we began to converse with each other and go on rides at night gazing at the stars. We would talk about life. He was intrigued by my guiltless nature. We eventually went on romantic rendezvous. We finally moved in together. He asked me to marry him and gave me an engagement ring. In my mind, I thought that I would go ahead and work on the procreation part. I just knew that we were going to get married. Before we could walk down the aisle, one of my family members offered me some advice telling me to be wary of marrying my children's father. I repeatedly pondered over his words in my mind. I ended up throwing the ring at my children's father. It wasn't until I had our children that I felt like God was taking the blinders off my eyes. I left my children's father and decided to raise our children on my own.

When I was younger, my parents were very strict and wary about allowing us to stay at other family members' or anyone else's house. Now that I am an adult, I see why. I had difficulties with the dating scene because I did not trust my kids with everybody. Even if people offered, I would not let them keep my kids. I felt as though it was my job to protect them. There were times when I took my children with me on dates. I let guys know that they had to accept the entire package if they wanted to be with me – kids and all.

Soon afterward, I dated a guy who knew my children's father's girlfriend. He was a gossiper. He would keep me informed on what was going on in my children's father's life and loved to be in the club. He was prettier than me. His hair looked better than mine. Unacceptably, he made an appalling decision to put his hands on me. That was the first and last time he touched me. He tried to get back in my good graces, but I wasn't allowing it. Real men don't hit women.

When my children were toddlers, I dated a guy who was a compulsive liar. I knew him when I was younger and he came back into my life as my children grew older. He had gotten married. He tried to assure me that he was no longer married. He called my bluff in going to the courthouse to prove that he was divorced. Needless to say, he did not know that I went to the courthouse on my own and found out that he lied about getting a divorce. I'm glad I found out before I entertained him past a mere conversation. Unfortunately, his life ended a few years later.

I recollect dating another guy. He was charming, but we encompassed different mentalities. He wanted to purchase a mobile home, and I wanted to purchase a house. He even mentioned buying the mobile home and then getting a house. I did not understand his logic and questioned his reasoning. Needless to say, we parted. I wanted more. I thought big even at that moment. I knew I needed someone who could see the same vision I saw.

I was in a relationship with a guy who lived out of state. He had three children he was rearing. Only two of the children were biologically his. I commended him for taking all three of the children. He was a Christian. When I was experiencing emotional difficulties with my job and my parents' deaths, he was supportive and always there for me. We had continuously discussed getting married. On Saturday, I would be ready to get married. But then on Sunday, I would not be ready. It finally got to the point that I said that I did not want to get married because I was too inconsistent. I also knew that marriage was not something that you entered into lightly.

I believed that he and I would have married if we did not have children. He had a son who was a behavior problem at home and school. That boy was seven years old and would urinate wherever he slept, whether it was on the couch, in the bed, or anywhere he laid down. One night, my boyfriend and I got into a heated argument about his son hitting my daughter over a necklace that did not belong to him. I verbally scolded him, while my boyfriend was sitting there. I was irate with my boyfriend because he was not saying anything. I was so upset that I grabbed a belt to spank his son's behind. Needless to say, my boyfriend stood between us. I reached around my boyfriend and struck him one time. He instructed the oldest son to call the police. I was livid. I grabbed my children and belongings and left before the police came. I was not going to allow him to destroy my livelihood. I had just begun working as a new teacher. Keep in mind. He had disciplined my children without my interference. That red flag noted a disaster waiting to happen.

Days later, he phoned me to tell me what his sister and mom said. They had asked about me. They even told him that his son was bad. Furthermore, they told him that his son was going to keep him from a relationship. If his mom and sister said it, how much more should I be saying it? I was unable to forgive him for instructing the oldest child to call the police on me. Eventually, we went our separate ways.

Subsequently, I started seeing a guy whom my hairstylist recommended. I ended up dealing with him off and on for over a decade. I always felt like he was my soul mate. I guess I was trying to wait for him to mature. When I purchased my first house, I remember I would always say that if you cannot ride with me on my canoe, then you can't ride with me on my cruise ship. He was always there behind the scenes. He claimed that he was ready for a family. Frankly speaking, he was not ready to give up his single life of drinking, smoking, hanging out with the guys, and chasing the ladies. When it came to him, I was so forgiving. I was oblivious to his shortcomings. He was a great friend to me. We always confided in each other. As a protective mother, I trusted him with my children. He would play with them and help them with their homework. When I moved, he reached out to me through social media to be informed that God had moved me halfway across the country.

As I matured, I slowed my role. I'm by far no angel. I have committed adultery with married men. Don't judge. Being gullible and naïve, I believed guys' stories about being separated and in the process of getting a divorce. Thank God, I became wiser. I learned not to believe those stories or lies anymore. I learned to do my research. It is true that "my people are destroyed for lack of knowledge..." (Hosea 4:6 NKJV).

I have been accused of being with people's husbands whom I have never entertained in any affair. I knew one female and knew that my platonic friend was her husband. She thought that her husband and I had an affair because we attended a football game together. Happy to say, I was not the culprit. It was somebody else who called his phone. It was not me. I approached her about the issue and eventually we reconciled our differences. I said something to her now ex-husband because I told him that he should not have mistreated her due to her past childhood experiences. By far, I am not callous and cold-hearted.

In my defense, I will say that when my children were little, I did date a guy who was getting a divorce. He even introduced me to his wife. His children and my children played with each other. We also went on out-of-town trips together. He had some great qualities, but our relationship was short-lived. After we had separated, I found out that I was pregnant. We were not amicable at the time. I ended up having a miscarriage. Father knows best. He allows things to happen for a reason. This guy was seeing someone else and disputed being the father. God saved me from a disaster. We also had dissimilar mentalities. I remember telling my maternal grandmother that these guys are not men but grown males. I said, "They do not have a pot to [tinkle] in or a window to throw it out of." I just knew my grandmother was going to scold me about my use of words. Instead, she said that I was just like my grandfather. I told her that at least I knew I had gotten it from somewhere.

During my children's middle school years, I dated yet another guy. He would always tell me that I was his wife, but God did not communicate that to me. God and I have a relationship, and He knows that I need confirmation from Him. I heard this guy's mom tell him that I was good for him. I told my paternal grandmother about how his mom had a conversation with me about us getting married. My grandmother noted how the mom loved me and how I should marry the guy. I let my grandmother know that I was not marrying the mother, but the son. The son still needed to deal with his past and mature spiritually. Years later, that same guy was still saying that I was his wife. One day on the phone, I mentioned to him all the horrific things that he had done, while we were together. After a long list of infractions and an indistinguishable silence on the phone, I heard the dial tone. I guess that was my answer, and his too. How can you say that I was your wife, but you did not treat me as such? You desired to hurriedly get me out of your house so that you could go hang out in the streets. Your actions did not gravely indicate that you were ready for marriage. I am so glad that God provided me with discernment and wisdom not to walk down that aisle.

Unfortunately, I dated a guy who liked to drink. He was belligerent when he would drink. He would call girls disrespectful names. He even jumped on my car and damaged it. I remember one time I was so fearful of him. I went into another room and got down on the floor and prayed. I told God that if He got me out of there I would not return. I knew that God heard my cry because He delivered me. Sadly, I think I went back a couple more times to finally never return.

And the beat goes on. I was at my cousin's wedding as a bridesmaid. Her brother-in-law was the best man. Unexpectedly, I ended up being in a relationship with the best man. It sounds like a romance movie. Similar to any relationship, it started like a fairy tale introduction. Driving back home from the wedding, we stopped at a rest area and conversed for a short time. The dialogue was impressive, and I felt a spark of chemistry. We parted as I detoured to spend time with my family.

Afterward, the best man and I reconnected. We enjoyed each other's company while attending a professional football game. We went to the movies. We traveled to out of town escapades. As time progressed, it declined. He was nonchalant, and that would frustrate me. We talked about marriage, but he was not ready for marriage. After we had separated for one day, I recollect a vision of a red car parked in his driveway. Of course, I went over to his house to find the red car in his driveway. I approached the door and knocked. He would not let me in. He just kept telling me that he had a friend in the house. I think that he finally admitted to being involved with someone else. We stopped seeing each other and then got back together. I felt as though he was continuously being deceptive. He was just so callous and cold-hearted and thought that I was supposed to easily forgive him. I felt like he deflected his actions onto me. We ended up going our separate ways because I could not trust him and could not forgive him. I allowed the situation to cause me to do crazy things. I wanted it to work. But, the trust was broken and could not be rekindled. He did not understand that once you break the trust that you have to work to gain it back. Without trust, there is no relationship.

I reminisced long after my maternal grandmother passed. I had a dream about her. In the dream, she told me to go to church. When I woke up, I took her advice soon after that dream. The closer I got to God the more I got away from the guy that I was seeing at the time. God knows when to send you someone you will listen to get you to where He wants you to be.

I entertained men through dating apps. I heard some success stories, so I thought that I would try it. God did not want me on those sites. I met with some guys to never see them again. Finally, I met one near my hometown. We would see each other by meeting up at each other's houses and dining out at various restaurants. Like all the others, it turned for the worse. My grandma would always talk about dating a guy from church, so I thought that I was safe. I thought because he went to church he would be better than some of the other guys. He was no better. Some of the men in the church are not any better than the ones outside the church. They are "church players" and carnal. When I say this, I do not reference all men who attend church. What I learned is that you have to date men who have a relationship with God and live a holy life.

Unexpectedly, this guy wanted me to help with car repair expenses. Why would I assist you with your car repair and I haven't even ridden in that car? Now, he has driven me in his other car. But regardless of which car, I felt like he should be a man and take care of his business. He thought that he was going to con me into helping him. I refused. I provided him with my dad's sage. My dad always declared, "A man will work two or three jobs to take care of his family." At times, he would get missing in action. He was supposed to spend time with me for Thanksgiving, Christmas, and New Year's Day. I had concluded that three strikes, and he was out. I had to call it quits.

To my surprise, this same guy suggested that we go to the beach. I took off two days from work. We went to the beach and had an exhilarating time. He treated me like a queen. Two days of pleasure, but more days of pain. He left me at his house and stayed gone for hours and said that he did not know when he would be back. I stayed at his house that night because I was exhausted. He was nowhere to be found. I had to let that relationship go. Months later, I saw him out with another woman. I cordially spoke to her and him. About a year later, I saw him with another woman. Let's just say, it was not my loss.

After dealing with all of these men, I had to be reminded of what God had said about me. The Holy Spirit said, "Can't just anybody get with you." It was confirmed over the years by men I attended church with. Even though I had that knowledge, I would still entertain guys that were not up to God's standards for me. I would date guys, and God would remove them from my life. Sometimes, I would be heartbroken. After a while, I learned to cope with God closing those doors. I learned to count it all joy.

The last guy I entertained for a short time did hurt me. I felt like God wanted me to provide him with my number. I heard a wise woman declare that God will give you what you think you want. She was so right because I did say to God he was cute. We attended church together. We talked and hung out. We had great times together. I even met his mom and the rest of his family, not once, but twice. We would hold hands. We spent time at each other's' houses. He even let his daughter hang out with me.

As time progressed, I found out that he was lying to me and the other woman. He was stuck on her and went through a tumultuous, toxic relationship with her to end up with her. I prayed to God about this situation. The Holy Spirit said, "He can't go where I am taking you."

It was during this time that I learned that I was a pastor's wife. God dropped a bomb on me. Afterward, I began to feel that peace that surpasses all understanding. He started bringing her to the same church we attended. I had to face my enemy. I would smile and wave at her. She would look at me with disdain. I saw them out at the park and heard him ask, "What is she doing here?" I acted like they were not there and continued to play with my grandchildren. I wasn't about to leave because they were there. I did not even speak about them to my family who was there with me. We respected each other's space and were civilized.

Fast forward. The Holy Spirit prodded me to purchase an automobile from a certain dealership. Lo and behold, who do you think was working there detailing cars? You guessed it. We were both in astonishment. The car salesman introduced us to one another, but he had no clue that we knew each other. I told the car salesman that we used to attend the same church. When I went outside, he spoke to me and embraced me. I told him that I thought that he would be married by now to discover that he was no longer with her. He realized that he had to make himself happy. He hinted at riding in the new car that God had blessed me with. Humbly, I informed him that I had moved to Texas. I left him with a somber look on his face. A part of me believed that he was regretful, but that ship had sailed.

I chose to have one last date before God moved me to Texas. Yet again, a guy from church approached me and asked me out for a date. We convened at a nearby restaurant that Sunday. Somebody should have warned me. He was self-involved and monopolized the conversation by endlessly talking about himself. I could hardly get a word in edgewise. He was loquacious about his past, present, and future. He even spoke about a past, maybe not so past, relationship with a woman who desired to marry him. Needless to say, he was impolite to the waitress. The waitress was courteous and doing the best she could. It was not her fault, and she kept us well-informed of what had transpired to cause the delay in us receiving our food. Unsurprisingly, I was turned off. Afterward, I saw him in church and grimaced. He came and whispered in my ear while I was ushering, "I don't understand why you don't love me anymore." Love you? He is preposterous. If anything, I was repulsed.

God was right in not blessing me with a husband at that time. I enjoyed being single. I did not like being with people who wanted to limit me. I remember telling my aunt that I was a bird with a free spirit. You could not put me in a box.

As God transformed me during the crushing and refinement process, I received His revelations. The Holy Spirit declared, "You will not go through what others have been through." That was refreshing to hear after I asked God why I was not married yet. It was in my singleness that I learned what God's purpose was for me on this earth. In your singleness, God will reveal His purpose for your life. When God provides you and your spouse with your purpose, then you will be ready for marriage. Marriage is a ministry. How can your marriage align with the will of God if both individuals do not know what their God-given purpose is? "Where there is no revelation, the people cast off restraint…" (Proverbs 29:18 NKJV).

CHAPTER 4

Adulthood

With adulthood, comes adult consequences. It was after my parents died that my world shattered. I felt like my life was spiraling out of control. I had the mentality that it was me against the world. How did the high school valedictorian end up in jail?

Was my mom right in saying that I was crazy? When you are a child, you do not know that there are things that occurred in your childhood that affect you in your adulthood. I remember countless times of seeing my mom and dad fight. When I was with my children's father, I would fight him. One day, he exasperated me. To frighten him, I discharged a firearm near him. The police came and apprehended me. I was charged with criminal domestic violence. I remember talking to the police officers on the way to the police station. I told them that my parents did not send me to college to place my degree on a jail cell wall. They asked me what I was going to do once I got out of jail. I told them that I was going to take my behind back to school and finish my education.

I think this was the time my siblings took a long time bailing me out. The jail attendants offered me a sandwich, but I did not take it. I was convinced that I was not staying there long. Next thing I knew, they instructed me to take a shower and put on the lovely jail attire they provide. We moseyed across the street. I was furnished with a pillow and some bed linen. The inmates were cordial. When I was about to receive assistance from the other inmates to make up my bed, the detention officer summoned me and told me that I was being discharged. I commented on the friendliness of the female inmates. The detention officer stated, "I bet they were nice." I was callow. I was so upset with my siblings for taking so long. In retrospect, I don't think it was them. I think the jail officials were trying to teach me a lesson. I knew that I did not want to be in jail. When I got out of jail, I expeditiously took my behind back to my college dormitory to focus on my education.

Ultimately, the court date arrived. It was by the grace of God that no one showed up to court. I have to mention that I was praying to God for some help. When I tell you that "God is our refuge and strength, [a] very present help in trouble" (Psalm 46:1 NKJV). Since no one showed up and I was the only one in the courtroom, the judge asked me how did I plea. Of course, I pleaded "not guilty". I was no fool. I thanked God for acquitting me. When God says, "No weapon formed against you shall prosper..." (Isaiah 54:17 NKJV). It was then that I knew God to be my lawyer in the courtroom. I didn't know that I had favor on my life. Be mindful that I had my children a month before this incident occurred. I had gone back to school because my children were premature and remained in the hospital. I ended up finishing my last semester of school and graduating.

One thing I remember is that I always knew how to pray to God when I entered detrimental situations. When I tell you, I look back over my life and see the hand of God in my life. He saved me and delivered me even when I was not doing right.

I stayed in trouble dealing with guys. I had a couple of run-ins with the law. In another incident, I made myself vulnerable and exposed my truths to this guy, and he went and told his children's mom. I was devastated. I thought that he was my safe place to vent about my situation. Be careful with whom you share your vulnerabilities. I did not take it well. I went and kicked his car and damaged it. I was so full of anger. My parents left us too soon, and I was not coping well. I remember the police coming to pick me up from someone else's house. I was so humiliated. At first, they tried to hide me, but then they decided that I needed to go with the police. I was charged with malicious injury to personal property.

When I arrived at the jailhouse, the presiding judge remembered me. I will never forget my bond hearing because he provided grace and mercy towards me. God had granted me favor with the judge. I ended up receiving a personal recognizance release bond, where you can sign to be released from custody with no money charged for the release. When the judge acknowledged me, another inmate became irate because the judge decided to be lenient with me.

Was it the judge, or was God using the judge as a vessel to bless me? Did the judge see the favor of God on my life? Once again, I remember going to court for another incident. That judge let me go. He told me that I needed to stay away from guys. Guys were always the cause of me getting into trouble with the law.

Around that time, I dated someone who knew about the expungement of criminal records. Nonetheless, I ended up pleading no contest and getting my criminal record expunged. I had to perform community service hours and pay a small fine. In retrospect, I felt like they should have made me take anger management classes. I performed my community service hours at a children's shelter. Incidentally, I began to perform volunteer hours there later on in life. Boy, how my world orbited back around.

After my parents died, I developed a wave of deep anger that I did not control. I did not exhibit the gift of the spirit of self-control. When God moved me to Texas, I put anger and rash decision making on the altar during my prayer time with the Lord. This was a time when God was sitting me down and allowing me to rest in Him. It was also a time when I realized that I wanted to give everything to Him. I became more transparent with God. Religion will make you feel condemned. The Holy Spirit said, "No condemnation." I used to be fearful to talk to God about my sins and issues going on in my life. I thought that God was disappointed with me. God is love, and don't you forget it. When you confess your sins and wrongs, God is just to forgive you and throw them into the sea of forgetfulness, but you have to believe. Your relationship with God is vital to your existence. People will lead you astray and cause you to be bound longer that you have to be. Talk to God. He already knows. He just wants you to confess your sins to Him so that He can provide you with joy and peace that surpasses all understanding. When you learn to trust and believe God, you will enjoy life more abundantly. I feel freer than I ever have. I have confidence that I have never had before. I trust God. He has increased my faith. He has helped my unbelief.

God "who has begun a good work in you will complete it until the day of Jesus Christ" (Philippians 1:6 NKJV). After completing my Bachelor's degree, I worked in various jobs. I worked at a manufacturing plant. I worked there enough to get my car payment and quit. I worked at another plant for them to release me because I was not fast enough to meet production. I worked as a teller at various banks. I was dismissed from one bank because I cashed a check for someone I knew after I was warned. I worked as an administrative assistant and data entry operator at various places. At one point in my life, I ended up working for a detention center as a warrant secretary. I learned so much at that job.

Finally, I decided to go back to school to obtain my Master's degree in education. My colleagues thought that I could not do it. I recall explaining to them that I could use my dad's military educational benefits. They disputed the idea. I just let them think what they wanted and resigned from that job.

Alas, the correspondence arrived in the mail. Was I accepted or not? I opened the letter. Approved. I was going back to my alma mater to obtain my graduate degree in the field of education. By this time, my live-in boyfriend was undecided about his future. I informed him that I was going back to school. We broke up, and he went back to his parents' house. A new journey began.

Now, I had to go through some wilderness moments. I moved out of the duplex I was renting. I had gotten approved by the housing authority to live in public housing or, should I say, the projects. I knew that I wanted to attend school full-time and work part-time, so I had to make some concessions. I believed that I needed to use income-based housing as a stepping stone to get me to where God wanted me to be. Living in public housing was not a pleasant experience for me because I was not used to those types of accommodations. As much as I hated it there, I survived. While dreadfully living there for over a year, I worked part-time at a school.

Being a teacher was a blessing and intrinsically rewarding. I remember when God opened up the door for me to go back to college. There were some ladies from back home that kept talking to me about becoming a teacher. I made the intentional decision to pray before going back to college to become a teacher. I have always wanted to become an attorney. I remember God working it out for me to attend college in the field of education. I was accepted. I was making good grades and just going through the motions. I did not come to terms with being a teacher until I performed my internship. When you are a teacher, the students come in with countless problems. I remember a student talking to me during a football game and began telling me her life story. After that, another student came to me with a personal problem. Avidly listening to their problems made me desire to become a teacher. I enjoyed being there for my students. I looked at my profession as my ministry. I knew that teaching was what God had called me to do.

I learned to embrace my situation like Paul and be content in what I have or don't have. I believed that when I became content, God eventually opened a door for me to obtain a full-time teaching job in another town. I felt like I had the favor of God. I was sending resumés everywhere. I did not limit myself to any geographical location. I received a call for my first full-time teaching job. I went to the interview and did not complete a job application form. After the interview, they had me fill out the application as a formality. At last, I had secured a full-time teaching position at a high school in the lower part of the state. My children and I were starting to see the light. Next thing I knew, my children and I were moving to a new town. We moved from the projects to a house.

Oh, what an adventure! I hated it there. At some point, I ended up having car trouble. I would put my kids on the school bus and walk to work. Advantageously, people would sympathize with me and give me a ride. It resulted in my principal picking me up to give me a ride to work. The struggle was real. No child support was coming in. I had just started my full-time teaching career after working part-time at another school in my college town.

The town was small, and the people gossiped just like they did in my hometown. These people also gossiped on the job. I loved my students. I just did not like living and working there.

After working there for a year, I went back to the upstate. An opportunity presented itself for me to return home to the school district where I graduated. I went for an interview. When I went for the interview, there was an assistant principal who was in the interview who was a high school teacher where I was a student. She spoke highly of me during the interview. She sold me better than I sold myself. It's like God had placed her in the room that day to favor me. I remember the principal asking me was I ready to come home. I said, "Yes." Before exiting, I confirmed my contact information. I finally received the call from the school district back home. They wanted to hire me, and I accepted the job offer. I was ready to move back home. I remember praising God and talking to both of my grandmothers about how God was moving me from the wilderness. I felt like I was going to the Promised Land. Ultimately, I worked in that school district for approximately 13 years.

After working there for a while, God blessed us with a house. I went from the projects to a house just like Joseph went from the prison to the palace. I remember when I purchased my first home. I had decided to purchase a house by a certain age. I was ready for my children to have their rooms, and we live on our own.

What God had for me; it was for me. That newly constructed house had sat there unoccupied for approximately a year. I recollect declaring to my maternal grandmother that the house had my name on it and that no one but me could possess the house. "The Lord your God will make you abound in all the work of your hand..." (Deuteronomy 30:9 NKJV).

Before that moment, my children and I were residing with my brother in my parents' house. It was challenging at times living with my brother. My brother was irresponsible and had quit his job. He and I did not agree on several occasions. My sister would add to the strife. She would tell us what the other one was saying about the other. She was not someone you wanted to confide in. To this day, I still do not confide in her. Nonetheless, I only resided with my brother to become more financially secure, make certain that I enjoyed my job, and ensure that I wanted to settle in that area for an extensive period.

My recollection takes me back to the moment when I told my siblings I wanted to purchase a house. They chuckled with unbelief. They thought that I couldn't do it. They did not know that "with man this is impossible, but with God, all things are possible" (Matthew 19:26 NKJV). When I moved, my brother did not help us. I felt like he was jealous. God sent a ram in the bush. Some people from church helped us move our belongings. Not only did I believe that my brother was jealous, but I thought that my sister was jealous as well. I had invited both of them to our new home. My sister did not know that I was informed that she had come into town. She and my brother got together and went out. When my sister returned to her residence, she called me to inquire about how to prepare for an interview. I educated her on what she should wear and how to present herself professionally. After reading the Bible, I learned that you "do not be overcome by evil, but overcome evil with good" (Romans 12:21 NKJV). It also writes, "...Love your enemies, do good to those who hate you..." (Luke 6:27 NKJV).

At times, I felt like Job in the Bible. In the beginning, my siblings would not come to my new house even with an extended invitation. Additionally, my children's father would not pay child support. I endured frustration on my job dealing with entitled students and no discipline for the privileged. I sensed that family members were jealous of my achievements through their actions or words. After attending a conference in Atlanta, a prophet prophesied to me that people were jealous of me. Beforehand, another prophet prophesied the same thing in a church in North Carolina. I could not understand why people were jealous of me. I was not a person that thought that people were jealous of me. As a result, I prayed that God would give me double for my troubles.

Over time, God blessed me with another house. Ironically, an associate and I were planning on purchasing a house or two houses together to rent. God's "thoughts are not your thoughts, nor are your ways My ways, says the Lord" (Isaiah 55:8 NKJV). Out of the blue, a tax collector phoned me about delinquent house taxes. I notified him that my house taxes were paid. He informed me that the property taxes on my parents' house were delinquent. My brother failed to pay the taxes. It was now his house because it was signed over to him. As I conversed with the gentleman over the phone, I noted that I would pay the taxes if the house was placed in my name. He said that I might want to discuss the matter with my brother.

I have to rewind. Before I moved into my house, God laid it in my spirit that He was going to bless me with a brick house with white shutters. While driving up my parents' driveway, I noticed that the shutters on the house were white. I never noticed it before. As a result, I met with my siblings to try and buy their share of the house. They refused to sell.

Once again, God worked it out for my good (Romans 8:28 NKJV). My brother ended up signing the house over to me in exchange for paying the delinquent taxes on the house. My sister and I conversed over the phone. She stated that if it was her, she would not pay the taxes and still allow our brother to stay there. Accordingly, I decided to move into my parents' house and sell my house. After pondering over that decision, I decided to take my other house off the market. I rented the house to a few tenants in an attempt to sell the house to no avail. I realized that God did not want me to sell my house. I prayed about it. He said, "A good man leaves an inheritance to his children's children" (Proverbs 13:22 NKJV). That was my answer. Today, my son owns that house. I always told my children that they could have their inheritance, while I was still living. They did not have to wait until I was dead and gone.

Time for a change. After becoming frustrated in my stagnation of working in the same school district as a teacher for over a decade, I decided to apply for other jobs. Finally, a door of opportunity opened for me. I ended up in another school district. During my four out of the five years of teaching there, I enjoyed my job. I would attend the students' games, performing arts events, and other activities while working there. Being in a high school was different from working at a middle school. They had varsity sports.

At this high school, they had Teacher of the Week for the Varsity football team. A teacher or faculty member could stand on the sidelines with the football players, participate in the team meeting, eat with them, and watch them run practice drills before the game. In the beginning, I would sign up for one or two games. But then, it got to the point where if teachers backed out of participating, I would show up on the sidelines whether I was invited or not. I loved being on the sidelines with the players. I no longer liked sitting in the stands with other spectators. Eventually, I started attending most of the games as the Teacher of the Week. God instructed me to be on the sideline for every game. In my obedience, I was designated as the Team Mom. I loved that role. If they would have given me a job to just work with the football players, it would have been a match made in heaven.

I stayed at that high school for five years just to become frustrated once again. I felt immobile. It was time to press into my prayer life. I fasted, prayed, and asked God to take me to the next level. The next level is where he took me.

I kept hearing promotion in my spirit. I thought that it was a promotion on my job. God had a better plan for me. It was not to stay at that high school. It was not for me to stay in that city or state. In my last year of teaching, I learned that promotion comes from God, not man. I could not fathom what God had in store for me.

CHAPTER 5

Single Parent Mom

Being a single parent mom was an intricate task at times. At the outset, I had no clue what it was like to be a single parent mom. I grew up in a two-parent household as tumultuous as it was at times. I had to learn what it was like to raise children on my own.

I remember when I visited my aunt in Washington, D.C. I discussed with her how I was not going to make my children's father pay child support. She asked me if I was certain. To this day, I still think about how my aunt asked me. She inquired in a subtle way that made me rethink my decision. After spending countless dollars on my children, I decided it was time for him to start paying. I did not conceive these children on my own. I reasoned that since he had fun conceiving these children. He should have just as much fun taking care of them, even if it was just financially.

When we went to court, the attorney had no knowledge that our son was named after my children's father and that our children carried his last name. My children's father requested a DNA test. Dissimilar to most females, I contentedly agreed to it. My attorney advised me that he would have to pay $800 for the test. With revenge as a motive, I had a desire to deplete him financially. I was unconcerned that he would have to pay $800 for the DNA test, half my attorney's fees, and child support. When we left the courtroom, my children's father called me in hopes of me dropping the child support. I just told him how asinine he was and how he was going to pay a great deal of money. I knew that he was the father of my children, so I was not distressed.

The judge ruled, and my children's father was ordered to pay child support. He hardly ever paid child support, nor did he get them on the weekends. I remember when he and I ended our relationship. I tried to discuss the children's future with him. He concurred, but never contributed to anything. My children's father was more of a hindrance than a help.

As time went on, I met this guy. He was helpful with the kids, but he did not work. Sadly, I became impregnated by him. I had gone on a cruise for the first time and drank some alcohol. My siblings and my children went on the trip. Little did I know, I was pregnant. I could not possibly be pregnant. I was so ashamed. I remember someone in church telling me that I was pregnant. I lied and said that I wasn't because I knew what I was considering. Before you knew it, I was having an abortion. Was I proud of that fact? No. I couldn't live with putting my child up for adoption or having another child with an irresponsible man and me carrying the burden of all the children by myself. I knew that family wasn't much help. I felt alone and desperate. So, I did what I thought was best for my situation.

After my brother and I got into a heated argument, I left. I hightailed it out of there and went to go stay with my maternal grandmother. It was crowded at my grandmother's house because some family members were staying there. When we arrived, they departed. When I got back on my feet, I discreetly disappeared while my grandmother went to church.

I relocated back to my college town. I ended up staying with a guy I knew from my college days. He went off to his military training during the summer, and I agreed to pay his bills for a month. I worked on becoming established while living there. I recall getting a white-collar job. Then, I started working at a restaurant as a waitress. While working at those two jobs, I obtained a job working at a delivery site. It was a decent job as a data entry operator. I quit the other two jobs, while I trained at the delivery site. I felt like I was not spending enough time with my children.

I remember one time I needed for my children's father to keep the kids because I had relocated. I was on my way out the door with my friends, and his girlfriend called. She asked me if her mom could keep my kids. I asked her about the location of my children's dad. He went to the club, stayed out overnight, and left the kids with her. Go figure! I told my friends that I had to go and see what was going on with my kids. I was frustrated. How are you going to leave our children with your girlfriend? I even recall some guys coming to my house and stating that they had seen my children before. I inquired about who had accompanied them and described their dad. They had no recollection of seeing him. They did divulge that they were with a woman and running around in the store.

I will never forget when I had to return to work around the holidays. I left my children with my brother in my hometown. I was in the car alone talking to God. I asked God, "How is it that he is riding around in a blue BMW and not taking care of his kids?" The Holy Spirit whispered, "Don't you have a roof over your head, clothes on your back, and food on the table?" I affirmed, "Yes." The Holy Spirit proclaimed, "Alright then." It was at that moment that my perspective changed. God was letting me know that He was my Provider who was supplying all my "needs according to His riches and glory" (Philippians 4:19 NKJV). All I could do was focus on what I was doing as a parent and not on what my children's dad was or was not doing. I even remember a time when I had car trouble and asked my children's father to pay child support so that I could get my car repaired. He snickered and said, "Ok." You know I never received that child support.

At some point, my car was repossessed. I walked out of my job one day, and it was gone to my astonishment. I had to depend on my colleague and taxi drivers to get me back and forth to work. I remember crying in the taxi with my children. One of my children wiped my tears and said, "Mama, it's going to be alright."

I met this guy. We decided to cohabitate. Don't worry. I did not get pregnant again. We engaged in preventative measures. However, I got to the point where I was unsettled and wanted more for myself. I remember two females from back home talking to me about a career in teaching. Even though I always wanted to be an attorney, I prayed about it. I was accepted into the graduate program for education. Afterward, my significant other and I no longer cohabitated.

My colleagues' dad worked at the housing authority. They convinced me to apply for income-based housing. I pondered over the thought. I was not raised that way. However, I wanted to work part-time and attend school full-time, so I swallowed my pride and applied. To God be the glory, I was accepted in a shorter time than was anticipated. That said, I went back to college. While I lived in housing, I would praise God to the top of my lungs. I detested living there, but I had to do what was necessary for me to attend school and rear my children.

The struggle was real. I recollect dropping my children off at their great grandmother's house for their dad to keep them. I was beyond exhaustion. According to the court order, he was supposed to keep them a week during the summer months. It was summertime. Before he could keep them a week, the police served me with papers for child support. I immediately hopped into my car and went to retrieve my babies. I almost got my children's father, his mother, and his grandmother for kidnapping. I had to go and get a police officer to accompany me because they would not give me back my children. They acted like they had amnesia. When the police officer accompanied me, they became healed of amnesia. His mom informed us that he had gone to the courthouse. I went to the courthouse to retrieve my children. I had sole custody. I knew that he was there because I saw the car he drove. While there, I informed the police officer that he was behind on child support. As we were going to retrieve the child support papers hot off the printer, my children's father walked in with our children. The officer provided him with some metal bracelets. Let's just say he went to jail for nonpayment of child support. Talk about things working out for my good.

We had to make a court appearance. I, the lawyer I have always wanted to be, came prepared with all of my paperwork. My children's paternal grandmother talked about how I had hit her. That was not true. She put her hands on me. I just wiggled myself away from her grasp. However, the judge informed her that the incident occurred out of his jurisdiction. Coincidentally, the presiding judge was the one who signed our child support papers. I began to read from the court order what it stated. The judge followed along on his copy of the court order and affirmed what I had stated. He asked me was there a time that I did not want my kids. Respectfully, I stated to the judge that there is never a time that I do not want my children. Immediately, the judge apologized and restated his question. He told my children's father that I determine when he can get the kids during the summertime. During the hearing, my children's father informed the judge that I was working and attending college. The judge inquired about my degree program. I proudly exclaimed that I was attending college to become a teacher and to acquire my Master's degree. The judge was impressed. When my children's father and I conversed after that hearing, I thanked him for making me look good before the judge. As a result of the hearing, my children's father had to pay back child support. It was like Christmas in July. Hallelujah! Won't He do it?

While on campus with my children, a guy inquired about me pursuing my college education as a result of me having children. I informed him that I knew that I could take care of myself with my Bachelor's degree and that my children were my motivation for obtaining my Master's degree to properly take care of them. Afterward, I received my Master's degree to teach Business Education and my initial teaching certification.

I worked part-time at a local high school. The teacher who chose to work part-time ended up coming back fulltime. I went to the lower part of the state seeking employment. I ended up getting the job without filling out the application. They loved me in the interview or were just desperate for teachers. I felt as though God had favored me. I obtained a teaching position in that district. I had interviewed in another school district. They would not employ me because I lacked sufficient experience.

I enjoyed the students. I abhorred my job and detested the actions of some of the people with whom I worked. I had to pray and press into the things of God. They loved to gossip and were meddlesome. I felt left out and that people were envious of me like I was a threat to them. I was only trying to make a living to support my children and me. I kept praying to God and praising Him. I remember complaining about my job to both of my grandmothers. I told my maternal grandmother that I felt like I was in the wilderness similar to the Israelites. Then, a job became available back home. I went for the interview. God is so good. The assistant principal at the time knew me from the time I was in high school. She spoke highly of me in the interview and sold me in the interview better than I sold myself. It was like God had strategically placed her there. When the interview concluded, I remember the principal asking me did I want to come back home. I confirmed that I did want to return home. He verified my contact information. Next thing I knew, I was hearing from the Director of Personnel. When I tell you, I yelled to the top of my lungs and gave God praise. I could not wait to leave. I was miserable and frustrated.

While residing in that region, I met a guy. Our relationship was short-lived. I became pregnant. When I met him, he made it seem as though he was getting a divorce and leaving his wife. I was so gullible. He reconciled with her. Truthfully speaking, I don't know if he ever left her. Once again feeling all alone, I had another abortion. Another unrewarding moment! I was ashamed once again. I felt guilty and condemned. With God, there is no condemnation. That was the last time I did such a deplorable thing. I had to ask God for forgiveness and repent. I had to change my ways.

I left the wilderness to enter into my land flowing with milk and honey. God blessed me to pay off my car. He also blessed me to purchase my first home. Nonetheless, my children's dad was behind in child support over $35,000. I remember he used to come to my house and ask me if I had cooked. Thank God I had read the Bible. He never tried to help me. He thought it was amusing that I was struggling. I remember telling another single parent mom whom I attended church with that I would cook and feed my children's father food that he didn't help me buy. I would allow him to enjoy the air and heat he didn't help me pay for. I learned to love my enemies and do good to them who were not good to me (Luke 6:27 NKJV). Yes, I looked at my children's father as the enemy. I knew that by being good to him I was placing hot coals on his head. Even though I was not where I needed to be relationally and spiritually, I would read the Bible and knew the Word of God.

In my prayer time, I would hear God's voice. Do you know what it is like for God to talk to you? Do you know what it is like for people to think that you are crazy for hearing from God and the Holy Spirit? I recall when God laid it in my spirit to get my doctorate. When I tell you that my money was funny, it was. I reflect on me peering through the window of the airplane gazing at the clouds in the azure sky. I was on my way to Phoenix, Arizona, to complete my doctorate residency requirement. I exclaimed, "God, if this is your will, you will take care of me." Lo and behold, when I arrived back home, there was a check waiting for me in my mailbox. God knows what you need even before you ask for it. The Bible states, "And my God shall supply all your need according to His riches in glory by Christ Jesus" (Philippians 4:19 NKJV).

During my journey as a mother, I would get frustrated with my children's father because he would not help me with the kids. I expected my children's father to be a stand-up guy similar to my dad. However, he was the total inverse. When I would call him to assist me with problems with the kids or adversities that arose, his response would be, "I don't know. What are you going to do?" In my mind, I would think what do you mean what am I going to do. I felt like he needed to be held accountable. He would praise our children and claim them as long as they were making Honor Roll in school and doing well. It's funny how absentee dads don't want to have anything to do with the kids but claim them when they are doing well.

On this journey of transformation, I had to forgive my children's father. I was tired. I tried to be accommodating. When our children were younger, I even offered my car, so that he could take our children to the fair. He refused. He had visitation rights. I would have the kids ready and waiting for them to be disappointed because their dad never arrived. He got them a couple of times, but not enough to matter. I told him that if he could not be a full-time dad, then don't be a part-time dad.

Absentee fathers have no inclination what single-parent moms go through. It is an arduous task to raise kids on your own. It was taxing on me when it came to rearing our children. At the end of the day, I would be exhausted. I still had to check homework and cook dinner. Except for the Good Lord, I was the sole provider. I remember taking my son to go and get his hair cut. I will never forget while I sat in the barbershop, a woman exclaimed, "God will take care of a house full of kids." That woman's assurance was timely. I felt like God placed her at that barbershop just for me. I have never forgotten those thought-provoking words even until today. I was struggling financially. As much as I would try to talk and reason with my children's father, he would chuckle and say he was going to help. Of course, he didn't. Then, he and his family dared to ask me to drop the child support.

As the years progressed, my children's father paid minimal child support. He was in arrears over $35,000. As the children aged, my son became a discipline problem. I found their dad and told him that he would care for him until he was 18 years old. Their dad took our son in.

It was during this time that I learned that you have to release to get the increase. Since my children's father was keeping our son and I still had my daughter, I thought that it was only fair that I drop the child support.

I prayed about it. As I prayed, the Holy Spirit instructed me to not only drop the child support but the substantial amount that was in arrears. Being obedient to the voice of God, I dropped all of it. You might think that was ludicrous. Strategically, a custodian said that God did not want me to depend on man and that child support, but on Him. I heeded the advice. As a result, I ended up with more. God blessed me with two houses. My children and I were sufficiently provided for. God told me to go back to school to acquire my doctorate, which increased my annual salary. My children and I were going on family vacations and experiencing life at a new level.

As far as my children's father keeping my son, it only lasted for a couple of years. He did not keep him until he was 18. His dad dropped him off in the driveway with his clothes, while I was not at home. Luckily for my son, it was a sunny day outside. His dad realized that parenting was not as easy as I made it look. After my son resided with his dad for a month or two, his dad received a call from a school administrator about our son being involved in a prank that he and others were engaged in that was harming other students. Needless to say, our son was suspended.

My children's father was always threatening to get the kids. I told him there was no way that any judge with any sense of reasoning would provide him with custody. After allowing our son to stay with him, an incident occurred with our daughter. She was supposed to mow the lawn and thought that she was going to be disobedient. Mind you, I had already sent her to a camp that was more than my mortgage payment. She was such an ingrate. She decided to walk off and leave the yard. I spanked her behind. She walked to her great-grandmother's house. On the way there, she scratched her face. Her dad and grandmother went to social services. I was accused of scratching her face and leaving a bruise on her thigh. I did spank her, but she moved. I reached for the buttocks area. Let's keep in mind that my daughter is not famous for telling the truth. My family and my children's father's family would always listen to my daughter. They would take what she would say and run with it. They didn't know that she was a habitual liar.

Since my children's father thought our children were so wonderful, the social worker advised me that I had the option to allow them to stay with him. Long story short, I obliged and signed on the solid line to allow him to keep the kids. The consent did not provide him with custody. Needless to say, their dad kept them. I was emotionally and physically exhausted. The case was unfounded. In my quiet time, God said that He was restoring me. God will bless you with a blessing so great that you will not have room enough to receive it (Malachi 3:10 NKJV).

I was taking flights, going on cruises, attending professional athletic events, and attending ballets and operas. I would show up at my family members' houses on a whim. I recollect showing up at my aunt's house and saying, "Surprise." My cousin said that she knew that I was up to something because I was acting funny on the phone. The sky was the limit.

As my daughter resided with her father, she did not come home one night. On Saturday morning, my children's father showed up at my door to ask me if she was with me. What do you mean is she with me? It was time for him to be a parent, so I let him. I laughed about that situation and joked about it to my family, colleagues, and peers. I took pleasure in seeing him sweat. About time. My children's father was negligent because he should have picked her up after the football game ended. He knew that she played an instrument in the marching band. What if the band director would have called social services? She admitted to calling him countless times to pick her up. Afterward, he acknowledged that he received the calls but that he did not recognize the numbers. So, he did not answer the phone. Since he did not pick her up, she went to a house party.

My children's father began to experience parenthood and began to realize that I wasn't such a bad mom after all. He also realized that the children were not as angelic as he thought they were. It was a wake-up call for him and them. My children's father learned through his fatherhood experiences to come in agreement with me, the matriarch.

As parents, we have to let go and let God. When I let go, both of my children returned home.

CHAPTER 6

When God Tells You to Move

In hindsight, I look back over my life and know without a shadow of a doubt that God was always with me. He said that He would never leave me nor forsake me. He loved me before I ever loved him. God knew that He had a plan for my life. I was so distracted by everything going on around me that I did not even have a clue as to what God had planned for my life.

I kept wondering why God was not blessing me in specific areas of my life. I would hear what He was saying about those areas, but I would not see it come to fruition. Little did I know, I had a purpose to fulfill. I did not realize that to get the best of God and His promises for your life you have to fulfill the purpose He has in store for you. God's promises are attached to your purpose. Other individuals were, as I thought, being blessed in those areas because they chose free will. When God blesses you, the journey is so amazing, and no sorrow is attached to it. I did not want my will to be done, but for God's will to be done in my life. God will take you to a land flowing with milk and honey – the Promised Land.

My daughter was always in some bind due to her poor decision making. My brother would occasionally ask me for money even though he was just as healthy as I was to work. I was always supporting the students at my school whether it was sports, performing arts, or any other extracurricular activities. I would work during the summer teaching summer school. I recall conveying to the students how blessed I was. One student said, "You are not blessed. You just work all the time." His words resonated with me. I would work extra hours during the school year trying to supplement my income as a homebound instructor and gatekeeper for the football and volleyball games. I was always active trying to make money to support my children. I felt like Martha when I should have been more like Mary, sitting at the feet of Jesus.

I kept hearing God say, "Houston." Initially, I thought it pertained to my cousin. I knew that she lived in Houston. Afterward, I volunteered with the prison ministry I was associated with in the Houston, Texas, area. I thought that fulfilled what God was saying to me. But then, I heard it again. I was baffled. Once again, I thought God was trying to tell me to visit my cousin. I still needed clarification. Time passed. Unclear about the timeline, I want to say that it was one morning before I went to work during my last year of teaching. I heard the Holy Spirit say, "Get ready to move." I heard it crystal clear. I thought God was referring to what He had already laid in my spirit that he desired to bless me with a new house.

During the summer before the 2018-2019 school year, I heard the Holy Spirit say, "Resign." I struggled with resigning because the school district had invested thousands of dollars to train me. I felt obligated to fulfill my commitment. Not to mention, I was the only teacher trained and certified to teach those classes. I had already recruited students for those classes, and they were looking forward to being in my class. I wanted to maintain a sense of integrity. I had also discovered that another teacher had resigned a few days before the school year began.

The school year started. I was frustrated. As much as I loved my students, I was ready for my exodus. I heard the Holy Spirit repeat, "Resign." God had let me know that my season was up at the current school where I worked. I remember saying to God that I did not want to be like Jonah in the Bible and how I wanted God to take me to another level. I had informed God that I wanted to be where He was. So, I began to press into my prayer time by fasting and praying. When you put those two together, fasting and praying are more potent. I have learned that some things do come by fasting and praying. I said to God, "This is the time." However, I wanted to make sure that I had heard from God. So, I asked God for clarity. As I spent more time fasting, I asked God when did He want me to resign. The Holy Spirit said, "Finish out the year." After much deliberation and confirmation, I resigned from my job on December 14, 2018, which was the last day the letters of intent were supposed to be turned in. With a letter of intent, you can let the district office personnel know that you are resigning. You can choose the date of your exit. I met with my principal and informed him of my decision. He was reluctant to accept my resignation and expressed his desire for me to stay. He notified me that I had time to reconsider before he would interview someone for my position. When I exited my principal's office, I was full of abundant joy and peace. I did inform them that I would finish out the school year. It took everyone by surprise.

In the course of me conversing with my principal, he proclaimed that he would support me in a conference, where I would be speaking. How many of you know that the enemy will try to stop you from your destiny? Due to some unforeseen circumstances, things changed. I informed my principal that I would still attend the conference because they were expecting me. I had already obligated myself. I ended up paying for the conference with my funds. "But as for you, you meant evil against me, but God meant it for good..." (Genesis 50:20 NKJV). I attended the conference, and my session was packed to capacity. "And we know that all things work together for good to those who love God, to those who are the called according to His purpose" (Romans 8:28 NKJV).

My level of frustration escalated that year. As the school year proceeded, we had students and a staff member pass away. Some students, administrators, and teachers added to my job dissatisfaction. Appreciatively, that frustration catapulted me into God's purpose and destiny for my life. I do believe that God sends people to frustrate you to get you to where He wants you to be.

One morning while I was fasting and praying, I was trying to gain clarity of why the Holy Spirit kept saying "Houston". While standing in my classroom, the Holy Spirit instructed me to move to Houston. I asked God, "You want me to move to Houston?" After digesting the information, I said, "Okay." That was me saying, "yes" to a bigger call on my life. Little did I know what God had in store for me. This task was bigger than my account, my degrees, and anything I could ever ask, think, or imagine. God called me from the occupation of being a teacher to His assignment for my life. Ironically, I recall stating to one of my colleagues that what God wanted me to do was bigger than the high school where I was working just the school year before. God will give you beauty for your ashes.

Well, how many of you know that the enemy comes to steal, kill, and destroy? In an instance, the glee turned into mourning. Unfortunately, this revelation came on the same day that one of my favorite students passed away. Needless to say, the enemy tried to snatch up that word. I grieved for a few days. I did not feel like praying, praising, or attending church. On the way back from taking one of my former students back to college, the thoughts I imagined were detrimental to traveling across a bridge. The pain I endured was excruciating. I decided to say, "Hallelujah!" a couple of times. After praising God, my strength was restored to where I was able to talk to God. I asked Him why He took my student. I heard the Holy Spirit say, "There is purpose in your pain." He also said that He was going to get the glory. I was so focused on the pain that I forgot about God's given purpose for my life. No one knew that this same student was an answer to a prayer by him being in my class.

On Sunday, the Holy Spirit instructed me to serve as an usher at church. I questioned God and told Him there was no way I could serve. In my sorrow, I was obedient. I served that Sunday. I was filled with emotions serving that Sunday. I thought that I was going to cry profusely in front of everyone. I was able to withhold my tears. A little girl touched my basket. It brought me some joy. At the end of the church service, the Holy Spirit instructed me to stay and receive prayer. God is so good. I began to tell the elder what had transpired. She prophesied to me and prayed over me with her husband by her side. As she spoke, God was doing a work in me. I thank God for those elders. I was on empty, but God restored and renewed me at that moment.

I finally decided to reallocate my focus. Do you know what it is like when God asks you to move from one geographical location to another? I didn't know what it was like to move from a small rural town to a big city. I realized that God's purpose for my life was connected to Houston. The summer before, God had already revealed that I had a greater ministry.

Over time, I let my students know that I was not coming back. I did not want them to be disappointed not seeing me the following year. Some students did not want me to go because they wanted me to stay until they graduated. Some students had been with me since they arrived at the high school. One student wanted to know what he was going to do without me his last year of high school. I reassured him that he would be alright.

I began to press in my prayer life and seek God as to what He wanted me to do. He sent me to an organization during my Spring Break. I felt as though God wanted me to reproduce that concept in Houston. I met with the director and he answered every question during and after the meeting. He also took me on a tour of the facility.

Finally, I traveled to Texas. On my journey to Texas, frustration set in while I was driving in the heavy rains from Louisiana to Texas. I asked God, "What are you doing? I know that you did not bring me this far to turn back now." I had to remember that after the storm is the blessing. I was stressed trying to get to the leasing office on time to retrieve the apartment key. We arrived with approximately ten minutes to spare. I felt like God was taking me on detour routes via the GPS to get me there on time.

Once I got settled in, I realized that I was in my Promised Land. Similar to Joshua and Caleb, I saw that the land was good.

God can use anything or anybody. Out of the mouth of babes, my grandson exclaimed, "Nana, let's go to church since you are so stressed." I thought it was a great idea. I'll have to admit I did not feel like attending church. I heard the pastor say, "God has appointed and anointed you for what He wants you to do." God knew what I needed. I was in the right place at the right time to hear the right message. Once I exited the house of the Lord, I was glad that I had been there. God is so good! That inspirational message brought me the confirmation I needed.

God had called me to something greater. I remember when God had me visit the juvenile court. I sat in the courtroom looking at the youths with their hands and ankles shackled. I became emotional. That could have been my son or daughter. I looked up and let God know that I got it. I knew what God was calling me to do. He wanted me to work with juveniles. While in the courtroom, God used me to tell a mom that it was going to be alright. She and I conversed for an ample amount of time. She blessed me when she told me that she knew that God had sent me. She confirmed that I was where I was supposed to be.

Before my cross-country voyage, one of the elders had prophesied to me and informed me that my assignment was in Houston. When I learned that this was my assignment and an Abraham move, I was moved by the words of the prophet. I was full of expectation, but fear crept in because of the unknown. Abraham left his family, country, and property. That is what God required of me. I knew that this was a move of God. The Holy Spirit murmured, "Faith. Blind faith."

One of the people I felt as though God was wanting me to contact to finance the God-given vision He had given me did not respond. I was distraught and somewhat frustrated, but I knew that God had something better in store for me. I began to praise and sing. Afterward, I heard the Holy Spirit say, "Something better." I had already been riding the day before to find a facility for God's vision for my life. While journeying and scoping out unoccupied land, I came to the belief that what God had in store for my life was something unimaginable.

When I moved to Houston, I just knew that I was going to get started on what God was calling me to do. Well, God's plans took me on a detour. God provided me with more than I could ever ask, think, or imagine. If we do not faint, we will reap a harvest. When God moved me to the Houston area, I felt like God was allowing me to live in my harvest season. Initially, I felt like Jacob, who wrestled with God, because I was so used to working. I was not used to God sustaining me and allowing me to rest in Him. God took care of me. It was my turn to live and stop taking care of everybody else. I remember when I prayed to God a long time ago and asked, "What about me?" God sees your heart and your willingness to give and take care of everybody else. A time exists when God will separate you from everyone. He will have you all to Himself so that He can bless you beyond measure. God allowed me to attend various events and go on shopping excursions. God began to connect me with new people who were trying to grow spiritually just like me. While at my new church, I learned so much in a short period. When I got plugged in, I saw my life transform before my very eyes.

I have heard people speak of their finances or utter other excuses for why they are not fulfilling God's purpose for their lives. God took me with my debt, fear, and other flaws. What people failed to realize is that God will cancel the debt. In your fear, He will help you with your unbelief. I felt as though God could not use me because of my past mistakes. I was imperfect. I had many flaws. I was allowing the fear of my past mistakes to keep me from my purpose and my destiny. With God, there is no condemnation. "There is none righteous, no, not one" (Romans 3:10 NKJV). If you are feeling alone, He will bring the right people across your path. In the midst of it all, God will have you minister to people about your journey. You will be an inspiration to others to cause them to pursue their walk with God.

When God says, "For My thoughts are not your thoughts, [n]or are your ways My ways" (Isaiah 55:8 NKJV). Believe Him. I felt like God was taking me on a detour. I thought I was supposed to get this juvenile residential facility opened. I felt as though we needed to quickly open this facility. Young people were still getting in trouble, and it was plastered on the news. I knew that God had a plan for my life, but He needed to deal with me first. Before God can do something through you, He has to transform you.

In the beginning, I resisted. I could not fathom what God was doing in my life. As time passed, I realized that God was refining and pruning me for what He called me to do. He needed to eradicate my sins and impurities. God will allow you to see yourself for who you are instead of the image you have projected yourself into being. We have been conformed to this world. Now, we have to be transformed by the renewal of our minds (Romans 12:2 NKJV). We need a mind of Christ Jesus. God will take you through a reset - the person God preordained for you to be.

God took me through a refining process of transformation. Just know that it was a ride of a lifetime and made me uncomfortable. There were times when I was anxious about what God was doing and not doing. You have to know that God is working behind the scenes. I remember when I was praying about my consultant's procrastination. The Holy Spirit dealt with me and let me know that I did not know what was happening behind the scenes. You have to be patient with God. You will reap if you do not faint.

Once I aligned myself with God's transformation process, the process became effortless. I learned that I had to be a willing participant. It is when I yielded, that God did a great work in me that brought about more joy, peace, freedom, and victory into my life. I was asking God to shed light amid my darkness. "If we confess our sins, He is faithful and just to forgive us our sins and to cleanse us from all unrighteousness" (1 John 1:9 NKJV). He had me asking people for forgiveness and granting forgiveness to people whom I thought I had already forgiven. When I thought I could get by with at least making the phone call and they did not answer, God would tell me to call back and leave a message. Sometimes, we think that we should not have to ask for forgiveness because we do not believe that we have done anything wrong. You have to engage in hard conversations with the people close to you and be able to listen to what they have to say. You have to let go of that pride. However, it frees us up. My period of transformation brought increased peace, joy, and freedom. There were times I would just find myself sitting in tranquility. I enjoyed my place of peace. Situations and people who used to cause me to respond emotionally no longer kept me bound.

During the transformation, you have to let go of some people. I was putting my anger, rash decision making, unforgiveness, fear, doubt, and any other sin on the altar. I was thirsting and hungering after righteousness. God had sent me to Texas for such a time as this, and I knew it. What I learned is for God to do something through you, He has to first get some things to you. You have to be cleansed from all unrighteousness. You don't want to get in rooms with your gift, but where your character will not allow you to stay. God is the Potter, and you are the clay. When He gets done, you will experience joy, peace, and freedom that only God can give. God will break every chain and anoint you. God disciplines those whom He loves. When he completes His work in you, you will come out as pure gold and not smelling like smoke. I am thankful to God for the pruning - the threshing floor.

When God had me asking for forgiveness, pride existed. Who wants to admit that they are wrong? I apologized out of obedience. God said apologizing was for me. Consequently, I attended a family member's funeral. One of the people I had to apologize to was in attendance. She was still unforgiving and holding a grudge. Her body language revealed that she had not forgiven me. She kept turning her back towards me. She would walk off when I approached the area where she was standing even while I was speaking to others nearby. One thing God showed me through revelation was that I was the light in the darkness. While I was unaffected by her presence, she was affected by mine. What happens in the natural realm, happens in the spiritual realm. Light drives out darkness, but darkness cannot extinguish the light within you. She did not realize that she was allowing me to determine her mood and her location. Still yet, I moved around freely whether she was there or not and kept smiling. It was at this moment that I understood why God had me ask for forgiveness. It was for me. I had so much peace and joy. I felt the freedom to move around and to speak. It's up to you to ask for forgiveness, but it's up to them if they want to forgive you. Sadly, people do not realize that they are losing when they do not forgive and that you have the victory. "The battle is not yours, but God's" (2 Chronicles 20:15 NKJV). What a revelation! After arriving back in Texas, the Holy Spirit told me to pray for my cousin, and I complied.

What I learned is that asking for forgiveness if not about you, but for you. Unforgiveness is a selfish sin because you only look at things from your perspective and not the perspective of others. Your perception of what happened and the other person's perception of what happened may coincide. You have to realize that actions and words affect other people in ways you have not perceived or thought about. When my brother asks me for money, I look at it as I have given you money, but I can't continue to give you money. What am I going to do when I need money? I cannot ask you for it because you are always asking me. To him, he thinks that my sister is supposed to be my family and is not there for me. What's funny is that people remember what you did not do for them, but they do not remember when you did do something for them. They don't realize that you are enabling them when you continue to do for them. When are they going to become responsible and accountable for their lives? In the Bible, it states, "If anyone will not work, neither shall he eat" (2 Thessalonians 3:10 NKJV). I'm just saying. In my brother's case, you have a wife and children. I am a single parent mom with two children with little to no child support. How does that look?

As I continued to work on what God would have me to do, I would set up appointments. God will take you out of your comfort zone. I was meeting influential people from various areas. There are doors that God has opened that no one can shut (Revelation 3:7 NKJV). The open doors were effortless to stride through. Individuals would meet with me and answer any questions I had.

There are doors that God has shut that no one can open (Revelation 3:7 NKJV). There were times when I thought I should include other individuals in my God-given venture to find out that they were not as zealous as I was about God's purpose for my life. I discovered that people might start on the journey with you, but will not finish or start at all. It is not to say anything bad about these individuals. It is just that we have different priorities. There were also people whom I felt could have helped me get further along with their knowledge but withheld information. One thing I do know about God is that all His promises are Yes and Amen (2 Corinthians 1:20 NKJV). What God showed me was that it was a closed door.

God provided the ram in the bush. When one person does not want to help, God will provide others who will help you carry out His will for your life. I prayed to God recognizing Him as my Source who supplied the resources I needed to carry out His vision. I thanked Him for choosing me and allowing me to carry out the vision.

While working on God's vision for my life, I heard the Holy Spirit whisper, "Seek ye first the kingdom of God." When you have done it to the "least of these My brethren, you did it to Me" (Matthew 25:40 NKJV). We have to show the same love, mercy, and grace that God shows us to others. When you are walking out God's purpose for your life, God might have you go to a fast-food restaurant and purchase 100 cheeseburgers. Being the hands and feet of Jesus, He'll have you take those cheeseburgers and feed the homeless who are sitting and sleeping under the bridge. While I was serving the homeless, I thought about how my family and I could have been in the same situation. Additionally, God might have you give money to the poor person standing on the side of the street collecting money for his or her next meal. God might have you give your leftovers from the restaurant meal you just enjoyed to a homeless person on the side of the street. God might even use you on your job to feed the students who are hungry in your class. God might have you minister to your colleagues who might be going through something. It might be a smile, or just saying hello to someone. God might have you give a colleague a ride when his or her car is out of commission. God will use you to hug a colleague who has just lost his or her loved one.

When is the last time you held the door open for the elderly or anyone else? When is the last time you prayed and asked God how do you want to use me today? What is your next step, Lord? Lord, how can I serve you and your people? As a teacher, I would pray with my students about their situations and declare positive affirmations over their lives as instructed by the Holy Spirit. God would use me to bless students with monetary gifts for graduation. He would let me know how much I was to give. "It is more blessed to give than to receive" (Acts 20:35 NKJV). The students would be in awe, but yet appreciative that someone cared enough to sow into their lives.

It is through your seeking, time reading, and meditating on the Word that the scriptures look differently than when you initially read them. In the first chapter of Genesis, I realized that everything that God made was good. As I was reading the story about Noah building the ark, the Holy Spirit said, "Follow my instructions." I had been told by the man of God more than one time that I had to follow God's timing and that I was getting ahead of God. In my mind, I believed that when I was idle, I was disappointing God. As time progressed, the Holy Spirit said, "Slow down" and "Rest in me". So finally, I decided to be obedient. It was in this place that I began to hear more from the Holy Spirit, pray, and read the Bible. I would read and ask God to let me know what He wanted me to get from the scriptures. I had asked God to stir up His gifts in me. I wanted to hear Him clearly. God began to allow me to dream dreams and prophesy to others. Remember, "you do not have because you do not ask" (James 4:2 NKJV). It was also during this time that I prayed that God would deal with me and remove any generational curses. It's as if God allowed me to vividly see the generational curses of my family. I decided that breaking familial generational curses started with me.

What do you do when God tells you to slow down and rest? "Come to Me, all you who labor and are heavy laden, and I will give you rest" (Matthew 11:28 NKJV). What I discovered is that God first had to do a work within me to prepare me for where He was taking me. At times, I wanted to rest because I felt weary. Some of that weariness could have been when I made choices thinking that it was God using me. Many years, God has used me to help others. Now, I just wanted to be able to rest for a while. You do not know how weary you are until God tells you to rest. After resting for a while, I thought I became indolent. Then, I heard some pastors proclaim that God is doing things behind the scenes that we cannot see. While I was resting, I would pray, praise, read my Word, and meditate on daily devotionals. Do you know what it is like for you to seek God in the mornings, and He tells you to rest? What does rest look like? I was also told by God to rest and enjoy life.

To my astonishment, the Holy Spirit told me to attend a professional baseball championship game, NFL game, concert, and Meet and Greet. God was sending me out to the masses. I began to think about how we are the only light that anyone sees and that everyone is not going to come to church. Just think if we, as Christians, never attended an NFL game, baseball game, concert, or Meet and Greet. Where will we find the lost? Yes, some people are found in the sanctuary of a church, but most of them are outside the church. God instructed me to attend these events opening my mind to new possibilities of souls being saved or just seeds being sown into others' lives. When you walk with God, you will go into realms you have never entered before as a Christian who has a relationship with God. God is not someone we should place in a box. Noticed I said we, including me. I had to change my way of thinking. Our mind determines our outcome. God opened my mind to new horizons. Our God is eternal and possesses infinite wisdom.

I recall listening to a pastor who referred to your place of blessing. Your place of blessing might be relocating to another state. It might be serving in a ministry that God called you to, on your job, or some other God-given task. When you ask and seek God and let Him know that you desire to go to another level and walk out His purpose for your life, He will help you get to your place of blessing. Before I arrived in Texas, the Holy Spirit had already directed me to a particular church where I knew that I was supposed to serve as an usher. At this church, I would attend countless ministry sessions. Each ministry had its unique purpose in my life and was helping to enrich and cultivate my spiritual walk with God.

Even though I was reading my Word, I reasoned that I could read the Bible more. The Holy Spirit wanted me to get deeper into the Word by using a commentary. I struggled with the idea, but I would occasionally use the commentary in hopes of using it regularly. I would listen to sermons online that blessed me as I was on this purpose journey. I could see myself in several of the pastors' messages.

Revelation protruded from reading God's Word. We always have to remember to acknowledge God in every decision and ask Him to order our steps. Moses went to God for instructions before he went to pharaoh. He was obedient and faithful. "Trust in the Lord with all your heart, [a]nd lean not on your own understanding; In all your ways acknowledge Him, And He shall direct your paths" (Proverbs 3:5-6 NKJV). Moses allowed God to order and direct his steps as he led the Israelites out of Egypt.

As I read Abraham's story, it applied to my life. I knew that God moving me to Houston was Him getting me away from my family. The year before God blessed me with more than enough money to pay off my car from training teachers. He also instructed me to save the rest. I asked Him what I should do with my house. He instructed me to let my daughter stay in it. Frankly speaking, I always wanted my children to each have one of the two houses God had blessed me with over the years. I always told them that I was the cup, and they were the saucer. They claimed they did not want the houses, until they experienced life on their own. I informed them that they could receive an inheritance while I was living and that they did not have to wait until I was deceased.

As I read the story of Hagar birthing Ishmael and the events surrounding their story, I said to God that I did not want to birth an Ishmael, but an Isaac. When Sarah allowed Abraham to have a child with her maidservant Hagar, it ended up being a problem that Sarah could not handle. Hagar and Ishmael were sent to another place. Even though God still blessed Ishmael, Isaac was the promise. I even thought about how God blessed the Israelites with manna and quail. Most of them did not enter the Promised Land. Because Joshua and Caleb considered the Promised Land to be good and did not let the giants discourage them, they were able to enter the Promised Land. What I have learned is that God will bless you while you are in the wilderness, but your blessings are greater when you enter your promised land. Everybody's promised land is different. God moved me to Houston, but yours might be right where you are. When I told people that I was moving to Houston, they talked about the traffic, the tolls, and how big it was. All of those things did not frighten me. I did not allow the giants to keep me from my promised land – the land flowing with milk and honey. They did not know that I have always wanted to move to a big city. I just did not know that it was going to be Houston. We have to learn to wait on God, instead of trying to do it ourselves. With a faith walk, you have to learn that God does things in an unorthodox way. He wants us to operate with Godly wisdom, not worldly wisdom. In my prayer time, I recall praying and asking God to make my way successful similar to Abraham's servant as he went to go find Isaac a wife.

When my faith wavered, God was still faithful and kept me. We have to just believe. I didn't know what that looked like. I felt like I would believe Him one minute. Something would happen. Then, I would doubt Him the next minute. God continued to show up in remarkable, unexpected ways.

I learned that you have to work your faith. "Faith without works is dead…" (James 2:26 NKJV). I learned something from my granddaughter. One Saturday, I told her that we were going to the fair. She looked at me sternly and rolled her eyes and neck and proclaimed, "Uh ah, we are going to the park just like my daddy said." Her dad had left. As much as we tried to convince her that we were going to the fair, she was adamant about going to the park. She stood on the words that proceeded out of the mouth of her father. She did not waver. She trusted him with all of her heart. Guess where we ended up that day? You guessed it. The park. I learned something at that moment. She trusted her father and had faith. She stood on that word that proceeded out of the mouth of her father. Wow! That's why we have to pay attention to the children. God can use anybody. My granddaughter showed us what unrelenting faith looked like. She declared it and spoke it over her life, and it came to pass. Look at God! Out of the mouth of babes!

After reading the story of Gideon, I learned that you cannot take a large number of people with you. You can only take a select few, who were chosen by God. Everybody can't go where you are going. I remember seeing this guy. I heard the Holy Spirit tell me to give him my number. It was short-lived and didn't work out. I prayed and God said, "He can't go where I am taking you." As God continued to bless me, I comprehended what He was declaring to me. That is when my career took off. God blessed me. I was speaking at conferences in major cities and on influential platforms.

You might not see it at that moment. When God moves people out of your life, trust Him. He has our best interests at heart. God had moved me to another level. It was more than I could ever ask, think, or imagine.

When God relocated me to do His will, he blessed my family and me significantly. People could not understand what had happened because I moved in silence. Everybody cannot handle your story. People were questioning my family and me about what was transpiring. Were they inquiring out of concern, or just being meddlesome? Some just want to gossip about you, whereas others can learn from your testimony. They did not need to know all the pieces of the puzzle. They just needed to see the outcome. I have learned that you cannot tell people your dreams. Remember Joseph. When Joseph told his brothers about his dream, they had considered killing him. They ended up throwing him into a pit and selling him into slavery. It still worked out to Joseph's advantage.

Why should we fear? Whatever we put our hands to God will allow it to prosper (Deuteronomy 15:10 NKJV). God was with Joseph when he was in his master's house and the prison. Potiphar placed Joseph in charge of his household and all that he owned because the Lord was with Joseph. When Potiphar's wife lied about Joseph trying to sleep with her, Potiphar had him arrested and detained in prison. While incarcerated, Joseph found favor in the eyes of the prison warden and was placed in charge of everyone detained in the prison. Regardless of what obstacles he faced, Joseph's dream still came to pass. His brothers still bowed down to him just like in his dream. I knew that despite what I might encounter that my dream was still coming to pass.

I think about Joseph's life and everything that he suffered. I felt as though my life was similar to Joseph's, but different circumstances. I was looked over for promotions to become an assistant principal. From one district to another, it seemed like opportunities passed me by. I look at relationships that did not work. I look at familial relationships where there was no strong bond. Division occurred in our house. My mom and siblings were on one side, and my dad and I on the other side. I would do the same things other family members would do and be treated differently. My children were disobedient. Their father did not help significantly in rearing them, nor did he help financially. God worked it for my good. I heard a pastor say that it had to happen. It did have to happen so that God could get me to another place to help save souls.

On this journey, you have to be careful whose voices you listen to in this season. I had a person who offered some vital advice, but I decided to seek God for guidance. I did not want to be like Josiah. Josiah listened to the instructions of a prophet rather than the voice of God. As a result, he died. I knew that God was omnipotent, omniscient, and omnipresent. Needless to say, God instructed me differently than he did. I don't believe that he meant any harm.

In view of that, never be jealous of anyone's assignment because you never know what they went through to accomplish and achieve that assignment. The waking up in the middle of the night, wondering if you are walking according to God's orchestrated steps and doing what God has called you to do. Seeking His face. Fasting and praying to get clarity from God. I had to learn to get the right prayer partners and be around mature Christians who would encourage me.

Sometimes, I had to be like David and encourage myself. I had to be a willing vessel to fulfill God's purpose. It was a humbling experience because God did not have to choose me. He could have chosen someone else. As long as you are willing, God will use you. One thing I learned is that you cannot talk to everyone about your vision, even if they consider themselves to be Christians. Everyone's journey is different. Everyone has different levels of faith. I'm not saying that I am better, but I am saying that I am different. I am the exception. I have heard on several occasions where people have said that the richest place is the grave. Can you imagine countless people who went to the grave and did not fulfill God's purpose for their lives?

Countless times, we see the end, but we do not see the beginning and the middle. What God has for you is for you and what God has for somebody else is for somebody else. If we all seek God's purpose and will for our lives, this world would be a better place. We all are working together as the body of Christ. What is God calling you to do? How are you helping to transform this world and mankind?

While on a drive, I stumbled upon six young men at the park. These young men were candid about their experiences. They talked to me about being in a gang. They admitted joining a gang for protection and security.

One of the young men conveyed to me how he would have to take cold showers at night and did whatever he could to help his mom. They were willing to talk to people if they were willing to converse with them and get to know them. These young men were very intelligent and possessed visions and dreams for their lives. They just needed the right circumstances. One talked about how he had gotten into trouble because he assaulted someone. Another young man confessed that he was disrespectful and used profanity with his teachers. They talked to me without hesitation because I was willing to listen.

This journey will have you torn between your will and God's will. At times, I struggled with separating myself from the east coast. I loved being in Texas, but I missed some of my family, my church family, and being there for my students. During your time of purpose, God will separate you from people, just like he did Abraham. It might be your family, friends, or church folk. I read in the Bible where God turned Lot's wife Sarai into a pillar of salt. It is not good to look back to the familiar. You will find yourself around old mindsets and human wisdom instead of godly wisdom.

You try to bring people up with you. If you are not careful, they will bring you down and take you back to the former mentality. God was taking me to another level in Him and from glory to glory. I had to let my past life go. God was taking me somewhere different, and it was good. How can you place new wine in an old wineskin? It will burst the wineskin (Mark 2:22 NKJV). When God moves you, He will take you to His purpose for your life. God will stretch you, and change your mindset. God's thoughts and ways for our lives are greater than our thoughts and ways.

I felt like the people I connected with before did not understand my journey. I remember hearing pastors say, "The worst folks are church folks." Well, I tend to agree. Some church folks are quick to judge. They provide you with unwarranted advice. At times, the advice they provide does not fit your situation because they do not have all the details. They don't realize they are only provided with one page of an entire chapter. They just take what you say and run with it. That's why I love that scripture in the Bible that says to "be swift to hear, slow to speak..." (James 1:19 NKJV). Sometimes, if not most times, people just want you to listen to them without providing them with advice. There are times when some church folks have provided me with advice and increased my frustrations with my situation. Then, I would have to talk to God, whom I should have talked to in the first place. Some church folks talk about community, but you cannot discuss things in your life with them. I like being transparent, but you have to be careful who you share your vulnerabilities with in your life. Everyone does not understand your life. It is acceptable to be spiritual; just be some earthly good.

God wanted to connect me with the right people. I had to let go of the wrong people. Don't get me wrong. No one is better or less than anyone else. It's just that God is trying to get you to a place where everybody who was connected to you cannot go. It is during this season that God will stir up your gifts. One thing that I learned was that we have to listen to God and seek the kingdom of God first. I prayed Proverbs 3:5-6 consistently and for God to order my steps. You would be surprised at what God would have you do. He might have you giving to homeless people, hugging people in the church that smell like freshly smoked marijuana, hug someone who does not know his or her true identity while you are enjoying yourself at the mall, serve at church in a specific capacity, give people money in the streets, or any other service tasks. When I would be obedient, the amazing testimonies of others would erupt from their mouths causing me to be emotional just hearing their stories. Their testimonies were the confirmations I needed to know that God had sent me.

I used to think that "to whom much is given, from him much will be required" referred to a man's conquest of me (Luke 12:48 NKJV). Then, I realized that it was God requiring much of me in the form of His purpose for my life. If we will delight ourselves in the Lord, He will give us the desires of our hearts (Psalm 37:4 NKJV). That means God's desires for you, not what you desire for yourself. As I matured in Christ, God helped me to realize that He places His desires for us in our hearts. God's desires for our lives are exceedingly better than what we fathom for ourselves. God desired to supply me with the promises He had in store for me.

Some blessings will come along the way. Soon after I arrived in Texas, He blessed me with a car that I flippantly asked for. "You do not have because you do not ask" (James 4:2 NKJV). I recall sitting at the red light and talking to God about how everyone else desired a specific vehicle. So, I asked for one. I asked for a car that was sitting at the dealership across the street. Lo and behold, God granted the blessing. I could not believe it. I struggled with that blessing because it was more than I could ask or think. As a consequence, I felt like God was preparing me for the blessings He had in store for me.

When you are walking in God's purpose, storms and opposition will occur. I remember when Abraham took Lot with him even though God told him to leave his family. Well, I tried to keep dealing with my family. Just like conflict arose between Abraham and Lot, it rose between my children and me. I believed that God was letting me know that it was time to let go. It was time for my adult children to be mature. Instead of trying to help me, it was like they were trying to hurt me. I remembered Abraham and Lot and received the revelation. It was time to let them go. When God wants you to fulfill a purpose, the people you used to associate yourself with now become the people you have to disassociate yourself with in this new season.

God would call me to fasts and have me read certain books of the Bible. I remember reading the book of Micah where it talks about your family being your enemies (Micah 7:6 NKJV). At the time, my worst enemies were my family members. When I left, my daughter was on board with what God had called me to do and was acting responsibly. Unexpectedly, my daughter started being defiant and rebellious. A situation arose with my daughter. The Bible reads, "For we do not wrestle against flesh and blood, but against principalities, against powers, against the rulers of the darkness of this age, against spiritual hosts of wickedness in the heavenly places" (Ephesians 6:12 NKJV). I felt like my daughter was allowing the enemy to use her to cause havoc in my life and be a great distraction. She decided that she did not want to pay the rent according to our rental agreement. My son and I thought that she had moved out. When my tenant tried to move in, she reappeared. While my son was initially willing to assist, he decided that he no longer wanted to involve himself. The police ascertained that I had used the wrong documents to unlawfully evict my daughter.

But, how many of you know that God has a ram in the bush? I prayed and He provided me with someone who was more than willing to get the job done. It pays to be good to people. God let me know that individual was willing to help me because of the seed I had sown in that individual's life years before. The Holy Spirit directed me to read the book of Micah. In the book of Micah, it speaks of a daughter rising against her mother and how a man's enemies are men of his own household (Micah 7:6 NKJV). While all havoc was breaking loose at home, I realized that the enemy wanted me to be distracted on my problems to steer my focus away from my purpose.

I knew that my daughter thought that she had won the war, but she had only won the battle. Ultimately, I ended up having to get the police to evict her. The victory was mine! My daughter did not realize that the same people who were in her ear were the same ones who caused her to miss out on her blessings and wanted her blessings.

God had already worked the situation out and had it under control. While I was praying in Texas, a young lady was praying about her living situation and for God to move on her behalf. God linked us through a mutual contact, and she moved in. The Holy Spirit had already instructed me on what to charge. Little did I know, it was what she was already paying at her other place of residence. God had heard both of our cries and answered us. She wanted a better place to live, and I wanted God to provide a better tenant. I was proclaiming to God that I knew that He did not bring me here for me to turn back now.

I felt like my children were trying to ruin me and wanted me to abort my purpose. What they didn't know is that mommy was spending time with the Lord reading the Word, praising God, communing with the Lord, and attending several ministry classes at church. Let's not forget about church service on Saturday or Sunday. I was getting closer to God. The closer I was getting to God the more the opposition came. Ironically, the Holy Spirit warned me that the storms would come. However, He told me that no weapon formed against me would prosper and that He was my Vindicator.

One thing I came to realize is that no matter what you go through, don't let people or circumstances change who you are. Love, forgive, and laugh. Do not let people or situations steal your joy. Stay focused on the things of God and what God has called you to do. Those other things are just distractions to keep you from your purpose.

People do not understand that trials and tribulations will come as a result of your obedience to God, not because of anything you have done wrong. On countless occasions, I have heard people say or think that people going through things has to do with their sin. Frankly, I have thought it as well. That is so far from the truth. What about when you are experiencing opposition because you were obedient to God? The enemy is after your purpose. He does not want you to fulfill your God-given purpose because he knows that there are countless lives and souls tied to your purpose. These individuals will be led to salvation and God's purpose and will for their lives. If we all would just get in position, seek God's face, and accept God's will for our lives, we can all live in Canaan. Canaan is the land flowing with milk and honey. We all could experience the promises of God for our lives.

Moving took me to a new level and dimension in Christ in 2019. I could not wait to see what God had in store for me in 2020. As the new year commenced, I felt myself gaining a new mindset. I was beginning to think big again. I was starting to believe again. I knew that without faith, it was impossible to please God (Hebrews 11:6 NKJV). I learned to praise God even more. If God has done something for you before, He will do it again.

You know it is perplexing for me to hear someone say that they knew what God had called them to do, but they were not doing it. His provision is supplied for His vision and purpose for your life. When you walk according to your will, you experience lack. What people fail to realize is that you have to be willing to be faithful over a few things before God will make you ruler over many things (Matthew 25:23 NKJV). I remember when God called me to the Varsity football team at the last high school where I taught. I said yes to God. I made certain that I rested well on Thursday nights, so I could prepare for the long day on Friday. I did not dread my assignment. I loved it. I loved being there for the boys. However, at times I questioned God about what He was doing through me. The more and more I attended the circle meetings, I knew why God had me there. Several young men did not have the presence of a mother in their lives. Some of these boys needed to see what a "mom" looked like. As God continued to use me to serve the team, the coach increased my responsibilities. He named me the Team Mom. I took this role seriously. I knew that I was serving as unto the Lord because He had called me faithful.

After everything you have done and the sins you have committed, you ask, "How could God use me?" I asked a similar question. We think that we have to be perfect for God to use us. When I look back on my life, I did some really bad things. How could God use someone who has been arrested, committed adultery, had two abortions, and committed other sins? What I have found out is that God uses what you have been through to minister to others. He does not call the qualified. He qualifies the called. "For many are called, but few are chosen" (Matthew 22:14 NKJV). You just have to say "yes" and be willing to submit to God's will and not your own.

To be used by God, you have to go through some things so that you can be relatable. If you have never experienced anything, how can you minister to other people? As God was dealing with me on various issues that I had to place on the altar, one thing I noticed was how God was using me during my transformation to minister to others. Sometimes, people state clichés, but they do not provide you with the details of how God has done things for them. How did He do it? Was it magical? Did you have to participate and engage in the process? Did you have faith? Did God take you step-by-step? Were you called, or did you perform the task in your strength and said that it was God? I have learned that faith without works is dead (James 2:17 NKJV).

I became cognizant that not everyone hears from God, but it is plausible for them. I learned that some individuals do hear from God. They just choose to be disobedient and miss out on the move of God in their lives. I asked God what made me different from others. He proclaimed, "Obedience." Obedience separates those individuals who choose to stay in the wilderness from those who choose to walk into Canaan, the Promised Land, or should we say "the land flowing with milk and honey". Unapologetically, I was overjoyed to step into this new invigorating territory where my blessings flowed. Not my will, but God's will be done.

I thought that people and things were keeping me from God's purpose and will for my life. When the pandemic hit, I realized that God has an appointed time. It was during the time of the pandemic that I realized that God was raising leaders, allowing His people to get in position, and allowing us to spend time with Him through consecration. God wants us to know His heart. His desire is for His people to learn what His will and purpose are for their lives. It was during the pandemic that I heard the

Holy Spirit say, "Step out on faith. Walk into your purpose." I planned to do just that. As I went to attempt to go and rent houses, the doors were not opening up. Landlords were not open to the idea of using their houses for helping juveniles. I felt like the enemy was fighting me hard, but I remembered what God told me to do. I knew that souls and lives were at stake. I knew that I had to press on. I finally found a landlord who would rent to me. Look at God! "I press toward the goal for the prize of the upward call of God in Christ Jesus" (Philippians 3:14 NKJV). I had to remember that the enemy only fights you for your purpose. But, I also had to remember that no weapon formed against me shall prosper (Isaiah 54:17 NKJV).

Printed in the United States
By Bookmasters